D0195123

MILL LIBRARY

THE HIDDEN INFLUENCE OF PROBABILITY
AND STATISTICS ON EVERYTHING YOU DO

NUMBERS
RULE YOUR
WORLD

KAISER FUNG

New York   Chicago   San Francisco   Lisbon   London   Madrid   Mexico City
Milan   New Delhi   San Juan   Seoul   Singapore   Sydney   Toronto

Copyright © 2010 by Kaiser Fung. All rights reserved. Printed in the United States of America. Except as permitted under the United States Copyright Act of 1976, no part of this publication may be reproduced or distributed in any form or by any means, or stored in a database or retrieval system, without the prior written permission of the publisher.

1 2 3 4 5 6 7 8 9 10 11 12 13 14 15   WFR/WFR   1 9 8 7 6 5 4 3 2 1 0

ISBN   978-0-07-162653-8
MHID   0-07-162653-0

McGraw-Hill books are available at special quantity discounts to use as premiums and sales promotions or for use in corporate training programs. To contact a representative, please e-mail us at bulksales@mcgraw-hill.com.

To
Mum, Dad, Grandma, and Evelyn

Contents

Acknowledgments

I would like to acknowledge the guidance and assistance of Grace Freedson, Michele Paige, Micah Burch, Kate Johnson, Steven Tuntono, Beth McFadden, Talbot Katz, and my editors, John Aherne and Joseph Berkowitz. My two sisters and brother made invaluable contributions as my most plain-spoken critics.

In addition, throughout this project, I was inspired by fans of my Junk Charts blog, www.junkcharts.typepad.com.

Introduction

This is not another book about "damned lies and statistics." That evergreen topic has inspired masterworks from Darrell Huff, John Allen Paulos, Ed Tufte, and Howard Wainer, among others. From the manipulative politician to the blundering analyst, from the amateur economist to the hard-selling advertiser, we have endless examples of what can go wrong when numbers are misused. Cherry-picking, oversimplifying, obfuscating—we have seen them all. This book takes a different direction, a positive position: I am interested in what happens when things go right, which is to say, what happens when numbers *don't* lie.

The More We Know We Don't Know

What will we learn from Bernie Madoff, the New York–based fund manager–swindler who impoverished an exclusive club of well-to-do patrons over three decades until he confessed in 2008? Or from the Enron executives whose make-believe accounting wiped out the retirement savings of thousands of employees? Perhaps we ought to know why the reams of financial data, printed statements, and official filings yielded few clues to the investors, auditors, and regulators who fell for the deception.

What will we learn from the Vioxx debacle in which the Food and Drug Administration conceded, five years after blessing its initial release, that the drug had caused ten thousand heart attacks? Perhaps we ought to know why widely available health and medical information and greater scale and sophistication of clinical trials did not spare Vioxx inventor Merck, doctors, or patients from overlooking the deadly side effects.

We ought also to ask why, despite having access to torrents of stock data and company reports, most of us have not made a killing in the stock market. Despite tallying up the nutritional information of every can and every packet of food, most of us have not achieved the hoped-for bodily downsizing. Despite heavy investment in information technology, flight delays and traffic jams continue to get worse. Despite detailed records of our shopping behavior, many companies have but the slightest clue when we call their service centers. Despite failing to arrest cancer in patients during large-scale clinical trials, beta-carotene and vitamin pills keep flying off the pharmacy shelves.

These examples reveal the unpleasant surprise that the modern obsession with measurement has made us none the wiser. We collect, store, process, and analyze more information than ever before—but to what end? Aristotle's wisdom has never been more relevant than it is today: the more we know, the more we know we don't know.

Stories of a Positive Nature

We begin to overcome these failures by examining positive examples of how enterprising people are making sensible use of the new information to better our world. In the next five chapters, you will meet engineers who keep the traffic flowing on Minnesota highways, disease detectives who warn us about unsafe foods, actuaries who calculate how much Floridians must pay to insure homes against hurricanes, educators who strive to make standardized tests like the SAT fair, lab technicians who scrutinize blood samples from elite athletes, data miners who think they can detect our lies, lottery operators who face evidence of fraud, Walt Disney scientists who devise ever-clever ways to shorten queues, mathematicians whose ideas have set off the explosion of consumer credit, and researchers who offer the best tips for air travel.

These ten portraits feature some special men and women whose work is rarely celebrated openly. The reason for this neglect is that their achievement is not of invention, for which we shower awards and accolades, but of adaptation, of refinement, of salesmanship, and of perseverance. Their expertise is applied science.

The Statistical Way of Thinking

For me, these ten stories ultimately merge into one: all of these exemplary scientists rely on the statistical way of thinking, as distinct from everyday thinking. I organize the stories into five pairs, each dealing with an essential statistical principle.

What is so unconventional about the statistical way of thinking?

First, statisticians do not care much for the popular concept of the statistical average; instead, they fixate on any deviation from the average. They worry about how large these variations are, how frequently they occur, and why they exist. In Chapter 1, the experts studying waiting lines explain why we should worry more about the variability of waiting time than about its average. Highway engineers in Minnesota tell us why their favorite tactic to reduce congestion is a technology that forces commuters to wait more, while Disney engineers make the case that the most effective tool to reduce wait times does not actually reduce average wait times.

Second, variability does not need to be explained by reasonable causes, despite our natural desire for a rational explanation of everything; statisticians are frequently just as happy to pore over patterns of correlation. In Chapter 2, we compare and contrast these two modes of statistical modeling by trailing disease detectives on the hunt for tainted spinach (causal models) and by prying open the black box that produces credit scores (correlational models). Surprisingly, these practitioners freely admit that their models are "wrong" in the sense that they do not perfectly describe the world around us; we explore how they justify what they do.

Third, statisticians are constantly looking out for missed nuances: a statistical average for all groups may well hide vital differences that exist between these groups. Ignoring group differences when they are present frequently portends inequitable treatment. The typical way of defining groups, such as by race, gender, or income, is often found wanting. In Chapter 3, we evaluate the mixed consequences that occur when the insurance industry adjusts prices to reflect the difference in the amount of exposure to hurricanes between coastal and inland properties, as well as what happens when designers of standardized tests attempt to eliminate the gap in performance between black and white students.

Fourth, decisions based on statistics can be calibrated to strike a balance between two types of errors. Predictably, decision makers have an incentive to focus exclusively on minimizing any mistake that could bring about public humiliation, but statisticians point out that because of this bias, their decisions will aggravate other errors, which are unnoticed but serious. We use this framework in Chapter 4 to explain why automated data-mining technologies cannot identify terrorist plots without inflicting unacceptable collateral damage, and why the steroid-testing laboratories are ineffective at catching most of the cheating athletes.

Finally, statisticians follow a specific protocol known as statistical testing when deciding whether the evidence fits the crime, so to speak. Unlike some of us, they don't believe in miracles. In other words, if the most unusual coincidence must be contrived to explain the inexplicable, they prefer leaving the crime unsolved. In Chapter 5, we see how this powerful tool was used to uncover extensive fraud in a Canadian state lottery and to dispel myths behind the fear of flying.

These five principles are central to statistical thinking. After reading this book, you too can use them to make better decisions.

The Applied Scientist at Work

These stories take a shape that reflects my own experience as a practitioner of business statistics. They bring out aspects of the applied scientist's work that differ substantively from that of the pure or theoretical scientist.

All the examples involve decisions that affect our lives in one way or another, whether through public policies, business strategies, or personal choices. Whereas the pure scientist is chiefly concerned with "what's new," applied work must deal with "how high," as in "how high would profits go?" or "how high would the polls go?" In addition to purely technical yardsticks, applied scientists have goals that are societal, as with the Minnesota highway engineers; or psychological, as with the Disney queue managers; or financial, as with hurricane insurers and loan officers.

The pursuit of pure science is rarely limited by time; as an extreme example, mathematician Andrew Wiles meticulously constructed his proof of Fermat's last theorem over seven years. Such luxury is not afforded the applied scientist, who must deliver a best effort within a finite time limit, typically in the order of weeks or months. External factors, even the life cycle of green produce or the pipeline of drug innovations, may dictate the constraint on time. What use would it be to discover the cause of an *E. coli* outbreak the day after the outbreak dies down? What is the point of developing a test for a designer steroid after dozens of athletes have already gained unfair advantage from using it?

Some of the most elegant achievements in pure science result from judiciously choosing a set of simplifying assumptions; the applied scientist adapts these results to the real world by noticing and then coping with inconvenient details. If you have read the writings of Nassim Taleb, you will recognize the bell curve as one such simplification that demands refinement in certain situations. Another example, considered in Chapter 3, is lumping together distinct groups of people when they should be treated differently.

Successful applied scientists develop a feel for the decision-making process: they know the key influencers, they grasp their individual ways of thinking, they comprehend their motivations, and they anticipate sources of conflict. Crucially, they repackage their logic-laced messages to impress their ideas upon those who are more comfortable with intuition or emotion than with evidence. Because understanding the context is so valuable to the applied scientist's work, I have included a wealth of details in all of the stories.

To sum up, applied science has measures of success distinct from those used in theoretical science. For instance, Google recognized this distinction by rolling out its famous "20 percent" time policy, which allows its engineers to split their week between pure science projects of their choosing and applied projects (with an 80 percent emphasis on the latter!).

More

And there is something extra for those who want more. The Conclusion of this book serves a dual purpose of consolidation and extension. While summarizing the statistical way of thinking, I introduce the relevant technical language in case you should want to cross reference a more conventional book. To illustrate how universal these statistical principles are, I revisit each concept in a new light, harnessing a different story from the one originally selected. Finally, the Notes section contains further remarks as well as my main sources. A complete bibliography is available at the book's link on my website, www.junkcharts.typepad.com.

Numbers already rule your world. And you must not be in the dark about this fact. See how some applied scientists use statistical thinking to make our lives better. You will be amazed how you can use numbers to make everyday decisions in your own life.

Fast Passes / Slow Merges

The Discontent of Being Averaged

Meter mystery
If no one likes, why obey?
One car per green, please
> —HAIKU ABOUT THE MINNEAPOLIS–ST. PAUL COMMUTE
> BY READER OF THE ROADGUY BLOG

Heimlich's Chew Chew Train
Good film, big buildup, nice queue
Twenty-second ride
> —HAIKU ABOUT DISNEY BY ANONYMOUS

In early 2008, James Fallows, longtime correspondent at *The Atlantic*, published an eye-popping piece about America's runaway trade deficit with China. Fallows explained how the Chinese people were propping up Americans' standard of living. The highbrow journal has rarely created buzz on the Internet, but this article beat the odds, thanks to Netizens who scrapped Fallows's original title ("The $1.4 Trillion Question") and renamed the article "Average American Owes Average Chinese $4,000." In three months, Internet readers rewarded the piece with more than

1,600 "diggs," or positive responses, which is the high-tech way of singing praise. Evidently, the new headline caught fire. Our brains cannot comfortably process astronomical numbers such as $1.4 trillion, but we can handle $4,000 per person with ease. Simply put, we like large numbers *averaged*.

The statistical average is the greatest invention to have eluded popular acclaim. Everything has been averaged by someone, somewhere. We average people ("average Joe") and animals ("the average bear"). Inanimate things are averaged: to wit, after the terrorist attacks of September 11, 2001, a security dispatch demonstrated how to "weaponize the average water cooler." Economic processes are averaged, as when a market observer in early 2008 proclaimed "the new hope: an average recession," presumably predicting a shallow one that would depart with haste. Even actions cannot escape: when Barack Obama's lawyer interjected on a Clinton conference call during the heated Democratic primary elections of 2008, the media labeled the occasion "not your average conference call."

Can rare items be averaged? You bet. *Forbes* magazine told us, "The average billionaire [in 2007] is 62 years old." Surely no one averages uncountable things, you think. Not so quick; the U.S. Census Bureau has devised a methodology for averaging time: on an "average day" in 2006, U.S. residents slept 8.6 hours, worked 3.8 hours, and spent 5.1 hours doing leisure and sporting activities. It is a near impossibility to find something that has not been averaged. So pervasive is the idea that we assume it to be inborn and not learned, nor in need of inventing.

Now picture a world without averages. Imagine having the average child, the average bear, and the average such-and-so-forth punched out of our lexicon. We are dumbfounded to learn that such a world did exist once, before a Belgian statistician, Adolphe Quetelet, invented the "average man" (*l'homme moyen*) in 1831.

Who would have thought: such a commonplace idea is younger than the U.S. Constitution!

Before Quetelet, no one had entertained the import of statistical thinking to the social sciences. Up until that time, statistics and probability fascinated only the astronomers who decoded celestial phenomena and the mathematicians who analyzed gambling games. Quetelet himself was first a distinguished astronomer, the founding director of the Brussels Observatory. It was in midlife that he set the ambitious agenda to appropriate scientific techniques to examine the social milieu. He placed the average man at the center of the subject he named "social physics." While the actual methods of analysis used by Quetelet would strike modern eyes as hardly impressive, historians have, at long last, recognized his impact on the instruments of social science research as nothing short of revolutionary. In particular, his inquiry into what made an able army conscript earned the admiration of Florence Nightingale (it is little known that the famous nurse was a superb statistician who became an honorary member of the American Statistical Association in 1874). In this body of work also lay the origin of the body mass index (BMI), sometimes called the Quetelet index, still used by doctors today to diagnose overweight and underweight conditions.

Since the concept of the average man has been so firmly ingrained into our consciousness, we sometimes fail to appreciate how revolutionary Quetelet really was. The average man was literally an invention, for the average anything did not, and does not, physically exist. We can describe it, but we cannot place it. We know it but have never met it. Where does one find the "average Joe"? Which "average bear" can Yogi Bear outsmart? Which call is the "average" conference call? Which day is the "average" day?

Yet this monumental invention constantly tempts us to confuse the imaginary with the real. Thus, when Fallows calculated an average of $4,000 debt to China per American, he implicitly placed all Americans on equal footing, spreading $1.4 trillion evenly among the population, replacing 300 million individuals with 300 million clones of the imaginary average Joe. (Incidentally, the Netizens mistakenly fabricated only 300 million Chinese clones, rhetorically wiping out three-quarters of China's 1.3 billion people. The correct math should have found the average Chinese lending $1,000 to America.) Averaging stamps out diversity, reducing anything to its simplest terms. In so doing, we run the risk of oversimplifying, of forgetting the variations around the average.

Hitching one's attention to these variations rather than the average is a sure sign of maturity in statistical thinking. One can, in fact, *define* statistics as the study of the nature of variability. How much do things change? How large are these variations? What causes them? Quetelet was one of the first to pursue such themes. His average man was not one individual but many; his goal, to contrast different types of average individuals. For him, computing averages was a means of measuring diversity; averaging was never intended to be the end itself. The BMI (Quetelet index), for good measure, serves to identify individuals who are *not* average, and for that, one must first decide what the average is.

To this day, statisticians have followed Quetelet's lead, and in this chapter, we shall explore how some of them use statistical thinking to battle two great inconveniences in modern living: the hour-long commute to and from work and the hour-long wait to get on a theme park ride. A reasonable person, when trapped in traffic or stuck in a long queue, will suspect that whoever was in charge of planning must have fallen asleep on the job. To see why this reaction misplaces the blame, we need to know a little about the statistics of averages. Working with engineers and psychologists, statisticians are applying this knowledge to save us waiting time.

~ # # # ~

To label Dr. Edward Waller and Dr. Yvette Bendeck Disney World die-hards would be an understatement. On October 20, 2007, they toured every last open attraction in the Magic Kingdom in just under thirteen hours. That meant fifty rides, shows, parades, and live performances. Buzz Lightyear's Space Ranger Spin, Barnstormer at Goofy's Wiseacre Farm, Beauty and the Beast—Live on Stage, Splash Mountain, Mad Tea Party, Many Adventures of Winnie the Pooh, you name it—everything in the park! Nice work if you can manage it, no? Disney buffs know this to be a mission impossible; they feel lucky to visit four major rides on a busy day, not to mention the nonstop walking required within the hundred acres of park area. Waller and Bendeck had help from Len Testa, who devised the Ultimate Magic Kingdom Touring Plan. Testa's plan lays out precise directions for reaching every attraction in the shortest time possible. He warns unsuspecting novices that it "sacrifices virtually all of your personal comfort."

Len Testa is a thirty-something computer programmer from Greensboro, North Carolina. As the patron saint of disgruntled Disney theme park–goers worldwide, he brought the gift of touring plans, which prescribe routes that guide patrons through a sequence of attractions in the shortest time possible. While the Ultimate Plan grabs attention, Testa creates touring plans for just about every need: for small kids, families, tweens, active seniors, grandparents with small children, and so on. He is mainly looking after rabid Disney fans, ones who are the most loyal—and easily the most demanding—customers. Sampling their typically breathless trip reports, posted on fan websites or relayed to journalists, one frequently comes across affectionate gripes like these:

> *"Going to Disneyland in the summer months is kind of like cruising to the Bahamas during hurricane season. You're just asking for it."*

"You haven't lived until you've stampeded to Space Mountain as the opening rope drops, alongside thousands of stroller-wielding soccer moms at a full run."

"When those gates spring open at 8 A.M., the weak and the semi-comatose will be left in the dust."

"We felt we spent more time in lines than on rides—the fact is, we did! When a wait in the line is ninety minutes and the ride is only five minutes, you have to question your sanity!!"

"I've never really forgiven my brother for that one time he slowed us down with an untimely bathroom break at Disney's Epcot Center five years ago."

These park-goers have plenty of company. Disney's own exit polls reveal long lines as the top source of customer unhappiness. Industry veterans say the average guest dawdles away three to four hours in queues during a visit lasting eight to nine hours; that's one minute of standing around out of every two to three minutes inside the park! *Amusement Business* estimated that the national average for wait time at major attractions in a theme park during the summer was sixty minutes—after which patrons get to spend two minutes on the ride. Since a family of four can spend $1,000 or more in a single trip, it is no wonder why some guests are irritated by seemingly interminable lines.

These trip reports leave vivid images of heroic maneuvers to avoid lines. A suitable attitude is required:

"When I'm in the parks, I'm a Daddy on a mission. . . . In the course of the afternoon, I'll go from one end of the park to the other and ride more rides, wait less in lines, and see more shows and parades than many other park patrons, with or without kids."

So are small sacrifices . . .

> *"We manage to avoid long lines with an occasional early morning, and hitting popular attractions during parades, mealtimes, and late evenings."*

. . . and knowing how to play the system . . .

> *"The mother behind me told me that they had waited three hours to ride Dumbo during their last visit. [This time,] she took advantage of early admission to let her kid ride three times in a row with no waiting."*

. . . and sweet-talking teachers into granting special permission . . .

> *"Taking your kids out of school [to go to Disney]. Is it worth it? Yes!"*

. . . and spotting opportunities that others give . . .

> *"It does rain in Florida, especially during summer afternoons. The good news is that this tends to scare off some people. My advice: Buy bright-yellow ponchos for $5 each from any of the gift shops. Then keep those kids walking."*

. . . while always adapting tactics:

> *"We are starting to think that reverse-reverse psychology might work: Disney opens one park earlier for all their guests so all the guests go to that park. . . . [Everyone else avoids that park, and] therefore we can go to that park because people think it is going to be packed and they avoid it."*

Queues happen when demand exceeds capacity. Most large rides can accommodate 1,000 to 2,000 guests per hour; lines form if patrons arrive at a higher rate. If Disney accurately anticipated demand, could it not build sufficient capacity? Did the appearance of long lines reflect negligent design? Surprisingly, the answer to both questions is no. The real culprit is not bad design but *variability*. Disney constructs each theme park to satisfy the "design day," typically up to the ninetieth-percentile level of demand, which means, in theory, on nine out of ten days, the park should have leftover capacity. In reality, patrons report long lines pretty much any day of the year.

Worse, statisticians are certain that queues would persist even if Disney had designed for the busiest day of the year. To understand this piece of anti-intuition, we must realize that the busiest-day demand merely conveys the average park attendance, and this number ignores the uneven distribution of patrons, say, from one attraction to another or from one hour to the next. Even if Disney correctly predicted the total number of patrons riding Dumbo on the peak day (which itself would have been a tough assignment), a line would materialize unavoidably because the patrons would appear irregularly during the day, while Dumbo's capacity does not change. Statisticians tell us that it is the variable pattern of when guests arrive, not the average number of arrivals, that produces queues on all but the peak days. Capacity planning can cope with large and static demand, not fluctuating demand. (A theme park that guarantees no lines would require capacity wildly disproportionate to demand, ensuring substantial idle time and unviable economics.)

The engineers who figured out these secrets are hailed as heroes by the Disney die-hards, and they work for the Imagineering division, based in several nondescript buildings in Glendale, California, near Los Angeles. They also design new rides, handling not only the thrill factor but also operations management. In the realm of waiting lines, scientists rely heavily on computer simulations as the mathematics of queuing are super complex and frequently irreducible to neat formulas. Think of simulations as turbocharged what-if analyses, run by farms of computers. Thousands, perhaps millions, of scenarios are investigated, covering possible patterns of arrival and subsequent movement of guests around the park. The summary of these scenarios yields reams of statistics, such as the likelihood that the Dumbo ride will reach 95 percent of its capacity on any given day. This creative approach to working around intractable mathematical problems was invented by the Manhattan Project team while building the atomic bomb and also forms the basis of *Moneyball* statistics featured in Michael Lewis's account of how the Oakland Athletics outwitted powerhouse baseball teams with much bigger budgets.

~ # # # ~

Wouldn't you know it? The same script plays itself out on our highways: the bane of commuters is not so much long average trip time as it is variable trip time. The statistics paint a harsh reality indeed: the average American worker spent 25.5 minutes traveling to work in 2006, and in addition, more than ten million people endured commutes of over an hour. In total, traffic delays cost $63 billion a year while wasting 2.3 billion gallons of fuel. But these scary numbers miss the mark. Just ask the pileup of readers who sent grievances to *Minneapolis Star Tribune*. Those truly put off by a long trip to work every day either practice avoidance . . .

> "*I chose to live in Minneapolis for transportation-related reasons: great access to transit and reverse commutes. . . . If people chose to live in Eden Prairie [an edge city southwest of Minneapolis], then I don't have much sympathy for their complaints about traffic problems.*"

. . . or have made peace with the inevitable:

> *"Every day, no matter how much traffic there is, it slows down right by McKnight [Road near Maplewood on I-94]. . . . There have been times when we have stopped and had a Coke somewhere because it gets so miserable sitting on the highway."*

Commuters know what they are in for, and they take charge of the situation.

If average trip time is not the source of bother, what is? Julie Cross, another *Star Tribune* reader, articulated this well:

> *"Picking the fastest route for my morning commute from Apple Valley is a daily gamble. Should I chance Cedar Avenue, hoping to hit free-flowing traffic for a 5-minute trip to work in Eagan? Or would Cedar be stop-and-go, making the reliable 10-minute trip on Interstate Hwy. 35E the better bet?"*

Pay attention when Cross used the word *reliable*. She knew well the average length of her trip to work; what troubled her was the larger variability, and thus unreliability, of the Cedar Avenue option. The highway route required ten minutes, with hardly any day-to-day variation. Now, if the Cedar Avenue option took five minutes without fail, Julie would never consider taking I-35E. Conversely, if the Cedar Avenue stretch took fifteen minutes without fail, Julie would always take I-35E. The only reason Julie Cross anted up each morning was that the Cedar Avenue route might take less time, even though she knew on average it would take longer. In general, if but one of two routes has variable trip times, then the bet is on. (See Figure 1-1.)

It is tempting to think proper trip planning will beat back any variability in travel time. But just like Disney's problem of fluctuating demand, this beast proves hard to slay. Jim Foti, who pens the Roadguy column at the *Star Tribune*, learned the lesson firsthand:

Figure 1-1 Julie Cross's Morning Commute Problem: Impact of Variable Trip Times

No Uncertainty			Daily Variability		
Cedar Ave. trip time	**I-35E** trip time	*Julie's* decision	**Cedar Ave.** trip time	**I-35E** trip time	*Julie's* decision
5 min. every day	10 min. every day	➡ Cedar Ave.	10 min. avg. (5–15 min.)	10 min. every day	➡ Gamble
15 min. every day	10 min. every day	➡ I-35E	10 min. every day	10 min. avg. (5–15 min.)	➡ Gamble
			10 min. avg. (5–15 min.)	10 min. avg. (5–15 min.)	➡ Gamble

"Last week, when Roadguy had his radio gig, he had to head out to Eden Prairie during the evening rush hour. Scarred by memories of backups at the Hwy. 212 exit, he allowed himself plenty of extra time. But the drive, right around 5 P.M., turned out to be as easy and graceful as a computerized animation, and Roadguy reached his destination nearly 20 minutes early."

Drivers find themselves in a no-win situation: arriving twenty minutes early leads to wasted time and even unanswered doorbells, while arriving twenty minutes late spoils other people's moods, wastes their time, and sometimes causes missed connections. This double whammy is on top of any extra time set aside in anticipation of traffic. And once again, variability is the culprit. Jim's strategy would have produced fruit if every trip were like the average trip. In reality, a trip that takes fifteen minutes on average may take only ten minutes on good days but eat up thirty minutes on rubbernecking days. If Jim allows fifteen minutes, he will arrive too early most of the time, and too late some of the time. On few days will he finish the trip in exactly fifteen minutes. In short, variable traffic conditions mess up our well-laid schedules, and that ought to upset us more than the average journey time.

~ # # # ~

After spending decades fighting average congestion levels, traffic engineers at state departments of transportation have come around to the paramount issue of variable trip times. What is the source of such variability? Cambridge Systematics, an influential transportation consultancy, has estimated that bottlenecks, such as three lanes dropping to two and poorly designed interchanges, account for only 40 percent of congestion delay in the United States. Another 40 percent is due to accidents and bad weather. Choke points on highways restrict capacity and cause predictable average delay, while road accidents and weather-related incidents induce variability around the average. They can create extraordinary gridlocks, like this one . . .

A truck carrying 45,000 pounds of sunflower seeds tipped over around 5:45 A.M. and blocked the left two lanes of the freeway for more than 2½ hours. Motorists encountered delays of 30 to 45 minutes as they tried to navigate past the scene.

. . . and this one:

A dusting of snow Monday was enough to snarl traffic on the freeways. . . . From 5 A.M. to just after 5 P.M., 110 crashes and 20 rollovers were reported on Minnesota roads. . . . A state transportation official had just two words for drivers: Slow down!

The unpredictability of such events makes freeway congestion unavoidable, and delay on some days considerably worse than the average. Not surprisingly, building more roads is the wrong medicine: supplemental capacity can eliminate bottlenecks, at least in the short term, but it does not directly affect reliability. Worse, many transportation experts, including economist Anthony Downs, warn that we cannot build our way out of congestion. In his book *Still Stuck in Traffic*, Downs elegantly espouses his principle of triple convergence, which postulates that as soon as new capacity gets built, commuters shift their behavior in three notable ways to crowd out any planned benefits: those who previously used local roads decide to switch back to freeways, those who previously altered travel times reverse that decision, and those who previously elected to take public transit return to driving. Thus, new thinking is needed.

The Minnesota Department of Transportation (Mn/DOT) has championed an advanced technique called "ramp metering." Ramp meters are stop-go lights installed on highway entrances to regulate the inflow of traffic. "One car per green" is the familiar mantra. Detectors measure the flow of traffic on the freeway; when the flow exceeds 3,900 vehicles per hour, the freeway is deemed "full," and the meters are turned on to hold back cars at the on-ramp. Another detector counts the backup on the ramp; when the backup threatens to spill over to the local area, the metering speed increases to dump traffic onto the freeway faster. According to an operations specialist with Mn/DOT, these controls temporarily delay the onset of congestion on the freeway.

Ramp metering has compiled an impressive record of success in several metropolitan areas. For example, Seattle saw traffic volume swell by 74 percent even as average journey time was halved during peak hours. Not only were more trips completed, but also less time was spent per trip! So incredible was this double bonus that researchers at the University of California, Berkeley, called it "the freeway congestion paradox." Typically, as more vehicles pile onto the same stretch of highway, inducing congestion, we expect travel times to suffer; conversely, with traffic moving more slowly, the volume of vehicles should decline. Such laws of physics seem immutable. How does ramp metering make its magic?

To unravel the paradox, we must first understand why the emergence of congestion is so feared. Statistical evidence has revealed that once traffic starts to pile up, the average speed of vehicles plunges, and oddly, the carrying capacity of the road degrades below its planned level. In one study, as average speed dropped from 60 to 15 miles per hour during peak hours, traffic flow dropped from 2,000 to 1,200 vehicles per hour. This disturbing situation seemed as illogical as if a restaurateur decided to lay off 40 percent of her staff during busy Friday nights, when one would have thought it crucial to run the kitchen at maximum efficiency. In response to the unsettling discovery, the Berkeley researchers recommended a policy of operating freeways at their optimal speeds, typically 50 to 70 miles per hour, for as much time as possible. In ramp metering, they found an ideal way to throttle the influx of vehicles, a means to maintain the condition of the highway just below congestion level. Its purpose is stamping out variability of traffic speed. The gain in terms of reduced travel time and increased traffic flow "far exceeds any improvements that could be achieved by constructing more freeway lanes."

And there is more to ramp meters. They also mitigate the variability of travel time. Two effects are at play here. First, metering ramps regulate speed, which leads directly to more reliable journey times. Second, the rule stipulating one car per green light spaces out vehicles as they enter the highway, and this dramatically brings down accident rates. Fewer accidents mean less congestion and fewer unexpected slowdowns. This is nowhere more widely felt than in the North Star State, birthplace of the notorious "Minnesota Merge." Jim Foti's readers again provided the color commentary:

"This is a personal peeve of mine, witnessing people slowly, gradually accelerate on to the freeway so that they just barely make it to the speed limit right at the moment they merge on to the freeway; this causes a conga line of people behind that first merger who end up arriving on to the freeway at 50-45-40-35-30 mph. Slow accelerating mergers can be almost as bad as people who stop at the bottom of the ramps waiting for an opening."

"[Where ramps are not metered,] groups of two, three, or more cars [are] TAILGATING EACH OTHER ON THE RAMPS, try to merge as a group. What the heck is wrong with their heads? Unless there are four or five car lengths between cars on the expressway already, how do they expect to keep cars in the right lane from braking?"

"The reason folks don't use their turn signal on the highway is that most of the time there is a jerk in the other lane who closes the gap so you can't get in. . . . [The person above] is 100 percent right. I no longer use my turn signal on the highway because of the gap-closers."

One reason why volume declines in concert with reducing speed is that vehicles get too close together for comfort when roads become congested. Some drivers are then prone to braking frequently, and in so doing, they release "shock waves" of reactive deceleration upstream, further disrupting the flow of traffic. Thus, the leaching of capacity during rush hours results from incompetence, impatience, aggression, and self-preservation.

Mn/DOT was one of the pioneers in ramp metering, installing its first meters in 1969. During a "war on congestion" in the 1990s, the network grew sixfold to become the densest in the nation, encompassing two-thirds, or 210 miles, of the freeway system in the Twin Cities metropolitan area. Mn/DOT is also the most aggressive among its peers at holding back ramp traffic during peak hours in order to deliver a reliable flow on the freeway. Industry experts regard Minnesota's system of 430 ramp meters as a national model.

~ # # # ~

At their core, both Disney and Mn/DOT face the scourge of congestion, and they have both come to realize that no amount of capacity expansion can banish the problem of variability due to fluctuating patron arrivals or unpredictable on-road incidents. Besides, expansion projects take time, money, and frequently political will as well as sacrifice from current users for a future, common good. Growing capacity is a necessary but insufficient solution. Statisticians believe that a sound transportation policy should emphasize optimally utilizing available capacity. Finding new ways to do so costs significantly less than constructing new highways and yields quicker returns. Ramp metering is one such solution. Disney managers have concluded that measures to optimize operations, while effective, also are not sufficient; they have gone one step further than freeway engineers. The crown jewel in Disney's operating manual is perception management.

- A body of scholarly research supports the view that crowd control is much more than a mathematical problem or an engineering puzzle; it has a human, psychological, touchy-feely dimension. A key tenet of this research—that perceived waiting time does not equal actual waiting time—has been demonstrated in multiple studies. Mirrors in elevator lobbies, for example, distort people's sense of the amount of waiting time; we tend not to count time spent looking at our reflection as waiting time. Accordingly, Disney engineers, or "Imagineers," devote a lot of effort to shaping patrons' perception of waiting times. By contrast, engineering solutions, including ramp metering, tend to target reductions in *actual* waiting times; these efforts may fail because people misjudge how much time they have stood in lines or stalled their cars.

Over the years, Disney has perfected the magic of managing perceptions. Take a walk around the park, and you cannot fail to see their handiwork. The waiting area of Expedition Everest, for instance, is decorated as a Nepalese village, with artifacts and flora brought back from the Himalayas; before getting on the roller-coaster, patrons weave through a yeti museum and encounter cryptic messages that generate excitement. At other sites, when lines get terribly long, "Streetmosphere" performers playing Hollywood characters mill around to entertain guests. Signs show estimated waiting times that "intentionally turn out to be longer than the actual time waited," according to Bruce Laval, a former Disney executive. The next time you telephone customer service and hear that computer voice announcing, "Your expected wait time is five minutes," contrast how you feel if a customer service rep picks up the call after two minutes with your mental state if you are still on hold after eight minutes. Such is the power of this classic strategy of underpromising and overdelivering. These and other designs suggest a briskly moving line or divert attention away from the queue.

The superstar of the Disney queue management effort is Fast Pass, the proprietary "virtual" reservation system launched in 2000. Arriving at any of the major attractions, guests can either join the "standby" line and wait then and there, or opt to pick up FastPasses, which entitle them to return at a designated later time and join an express lane. Since the FastPass lane always clears at a much higher rate than the standby line, the typical wait will be five minutes or less when FastPass holders resurface during the preassigned time. To aid guests in their decision, Disney posts the estimated wait time for those choosing the standby line, juxtaposed with the FastPass return time. Testimony from satisfied patrons points to the unmistakable success of this concept. One analytically minded fan, Allan Jayne Jr., demonstrated why:

> *"How effective is FastPass? Very. . . . Let's say that FastPass forced the regular ('standby line') riders to wait on average 1½ hours each instead of 1 hour while FastPass riders don't wait at all. So we have 9,000 people who did not spend any time waiting and 3,000 riders who waited an average of 1½ hours each for a total wait of 4,500 hours. That is about six months of waiting compared with 16 months without FastPass [all 12,000 riders waiting 1 hour each]. Thus FastPass saved ten months of standing in line!"*

Satisfied guests are eager to pass along their wisdom, as Julie Neal did on her blog:

How to Get the Most from FastPass

1. Designate someone as your FastPass supervisor. This person will hold all your park tickets, go off to get FastPasses for your entire party throughout the day, and watch the time. Hello, Dad?
2. Always hold at least one FastPass, so you're always "on the clock" for at least one attraction. Get one when you get in the park, then others as often as possible throughout the day.
3. Don't sweat it if you miss the return time. Disney rarely enforces it, as long as you use your ticket the same day it was issued.
4. Use the service for every FastPass attraction except those you'll be riding before 10 A.M. or very late at night.

Clearly, FastPass users love the product—but how much waiting time can they save? Amazingly, the answer is *none*; they spend the same amount of time waiting for popular rides with or without FastPass! It is mistaken to think that FastPass eliminates waiting, as the above quotation suggested; it is just that instead of standing in line and in the elements, patrons are set free to indulge in other activities, whether on less popular rides or in restaurants, bathrooms, hotel beds, spas, or shops. The time in queue, which is the lag between arriving at the ride to pick up a FastPass ticket and actually getting on the ride, may in fact be even longer than before. Given that the attractions have the same capacities with or without FastPasses, it is just not possible to accommodate more guests by merely introducing a reservation system. So Disney confirms yet again that perception trumps reality. The FastPass concept is an absolute stroke of genius; it utterly changes perceived waiting times and has made many, many park-goers very, very giddy.

Behind the scenes, statisticians run the FastPass system through a network of computers that count visitors and record wait times. When a new guest arrives, they figure out how long the ride would take to serve all the patrons in front of him or her, including the "virtual" ones now scattered around the park holding dearly to their FastPass tickets. The guest is then advised a return time later in the day. The line looks short but only because many people in line are not physically present. The new guest does not get to skip ahead. In effect, Disney presents park-goers the Julie Cross gamble: should they accept the *reliable* FastPass option, or should they get in the standby line and roll the die? Those in the standby line can get in with minimal waits if they happen to catch a lull in guest arrivals or FastPass returns, but more often than not, they will suffer hour-plus waits, as the following frustrated patron could attest:

"After standing in line for Peter Pan last summer for over an hour watching the FastPass line moving through constantly, it appeared that the Cast Members were more inclined to let the FastPass holders have far too much precedence over those of us who were sweating profusely (not to mention not smelling too great after a day at the park). It was aggravating."

Compare that experience with this view from the other line:

"A lot of people were trying to figure out who we were. You could feel their stares."

Like ramp metering, FastPass also works by stamping out variability, in that guests are being spaced out as they arrive. When the rate of arrival exceeds the ride's capacity, those picking up

FastPasses agree to return later in the day. At other times, when demand lapses temporarily, standby guests are admitted readily to prevent idle time. In this way, the rides run at full capacity whenever possible. As Professor Dick Larson, tellingly known as "Dr. Queue," remarked, "Even though Disney's theme park lines get longer each year, customer satisfaction, as measured by exit polls, continues to rise."

~ # # # ~

Back in Minnesota, perception trumped reality once more: much to the chagrin of Mn/DOT, the transportation department's prized ramp-metering strategy was under siege in the fall of 2000. State senator Dick Day led a charge to abolish the nationally recognized program, portraying it as part of the problem, not the solution. In his view, decades of ramp metering had come to naught as the Twin Cities continued to be among the most congested in America. The state came dead last, with 71 percent of its urban freeways declared congested in a report by the American Society of Civil Engineers.

Leave it to Senator Day to speak the minds of "average Joes"—the people he meets at coffee shops, county fairs, summer parades, and the stock car races he loves. He saw ramp metering as a symbol of Big Government strangling our liberty: "It's always bothered me—who stops? Who is the first person to stop at a ramp meter in the morning? Why does he stop? He should just go right through it. The first guy is jamming it up, and it ripples back to fifteen to twenty cars." How the senator managed to tap into a deep well of discontent! The *Star Tribune* readers offered their firsthand accounts:

> *"The operation of the meters makes no sense. Far too often the meters are on when the traffic is actually very light on the freeway, and in addition, the meters are cycling at a very slow rate."*

"Why do traffic managers allow the meters to create long lines at 6 P.M. when there are about thirty cars on the freeway and they are moving at 75 miles per hour? What's up with that? Is no one minding the store?"

Recall that Disney guests perceived their waiting times to have shortened drastically even though in reality they may have increased. In the Twin Cities, drivers perceived their trip times to have lengthened even though in reality they have probably decreased. Thus, when in September 2000, the state legislature passed a mandate requiring Mn/DOT to conduct a "meters shut-off" experiment, the engineers were stunned and disillusioned. They were certain that under their watch, the freeway system was carrying more vehicles per hour than ever before, and it was performing close to capacity even during peak hours because of ramp metering. They also knew most drivers were experiencing shorter total trip times despite having stopped at on-ramps. All the engineers got for doing their job well was a slap in the face.

The state extinguished all 430 ramp lights for six weeks. Traffic conditions were measured before and during the shutoff experiment to determine the effect of ramp metering. Cambridge Systematics, which conducted the study, collected objective data from detectors and cameras as well as subjective data from focus groups and a phone survey. On the eve of the metering holiday, the two sides issued dueling predictions of doom. Rich Lau, one of the foremost experts on ramp metering at Mn/DOT, predicted that driving without meters would be a lot like "driving in a snowstorm." He warned, "Any legislator who voted for [the meters shutoff] would have to answer to folks within a couple of weeks. The telephones would not quit ringing." Meanwhile, Senator Day also had a forecast: "I'll tell you when the disaster is going to be—a month from now, when they put them back on."

Soon, all of the Twin Cities' 1.4 million commuters took sides. As then House Majority Leader Tim Pawlenty remarked, "When we talk to people, they want to talk mostly about [Governor Jesse] Ventura and ramp meters." With few exceptions, they voiced their views, blissfully projecting their experience onto others:

"It was a dream. My travel time was a bit quicker than usual. I knew those meters were a hoax!"

"My commute [time] more than doubled today [after the meters were turned off]. I eventually had to get off 169 and take back streets to get to work twenty minutes late. Already I was going to have to move up the time I depart my house in the morning about twenty-five minutes."

"After experiencing life without meters, it seems ludicrous to me to consider going back to the same system."

"I think the meters should be fully returned to service after the monitoring period is up—no ifs, ands, or buts."

"When I'm leaving town at night, I wish the meter was there because it's too much congestion. They [other drivers] don't want to let you merge in. But at the other end in the morning, I save ten minutes [without meters]."

In the final analysis, the engineering vision triumphed. Freeway conditions indeed worsened after the ramp meters went off. The key findings, based on actual measurements, were as follows:

- Peak freeway volume dropped by 9 percent.
- Travel times rose by 22 percent, and reliability deteriorated.
- Travel speeds declined by 7 percent.
- The number of crashes during merges jumped by 26 percent.

The consultants further estimated that the benefits of ramp metering outweighed costs by five to one.

More important, the engineers did get that slap in the face, hard. The subjective portion of the study, reflecting public opinion, substantively replicated the rants by *Star Tribune* readers over the years. It was only now that the engineers acknowledged their blind spot. As Marc Cutler of Cambridge Systematics concluded, "In general, people don't like to wait for anything. They don't like to wait for a bus; they don't like to be on hold on the telephone. They tend to feel trapped and experience a lack of choice and control." In other words, despite the reality that commuters shortened their journeys if they waited their turns at the ramps, the drivers did not perceive the trade-off to be beneficial; they insisted that they would rather be moving slowly on the freeway than coming to a standstill at the ramp. At long last, the engineers listened. When they turned the lights back on, they limited waiting time on the ramps to four minutes, retired some unnecessary meters, and also shortened the operating hours. That was not the optimal engineering solution, obviously, but what the people wanted was what they got. Cutler continued, "There's a tolerance limit people have for waiting at ramp meters. That public perception has to be taken into account by government. You can't make decisions simply on engineering and planning principles." In this respect, the freeway engineers could take a cue from Disney's exemplary effort in perception management.

Dr. Queue, the professor who studies Disney lines, has a theory about this apparently irrational behavior. He has long advocated that traditional scientific studies of queues include the psychological perspective. What bothers people most turns out to be "slips and skips": being held up by a ramp meter while other cars zoom past suggests to them a grave social injustice. As one Twin Cities commuter lamented:

"Every day, I queue up and wait. . . . In my attempt to be a good responsible citizen, I just accept my fate. Meanwhile, I watch one [single driver] after another zip up the HOV [High-Occupancy-Vehicle] lane."

Of course, we have heard similar sentiments in the Disney standby lines.

~ # # # ~

The average man is one of the few inventions by statisticians that have found a permanent place in our popular lexicon. Statisticians use the concept in an altogether different way from the rest of us: they focus on the variations around the average, rather than the average value itself. For example, theme park–goers who worry about hour-long queues and workers who grumble about hour-long commutes are describing their experiences in terms of average waiting times. Statisticians tell us that large variability around these averages, due to fluctuating guest arrivals or happenstance, is the primary source of irritation. Such variations disrupt our well-laid schedules. Thus, the most effective measures for managing lines and freeway traffic, including Disney's FastPass virtual reservation system and Mn/DOT's ramp metering, aim to take variability out of the system. One may think that queues at theme parks can be obviated by expanding capacity, and that congestion at rush hours can be contained by building more roads. Such tactics are hardly sufficient in the face of variability. That, in short, is the discontent of being averaged.

2

Bagged Spinach / Bad Score

The Virtue of Being Wrong

> *You can tell a little thing from a big thing. What's very hard to do is to tell a little thing from nothing at all.*
> MICHAEL THUN, EPIDEMIOLOGIST

> *Does God only send hail to damage the roofs of people who are bad credit risks?*
> —STEVEN WOLENS, FORMER TEXAS STATE REPRESENTATIVE

There is a particular breed of statisticians called *modelers*. Think of modelers as reconnoiterers sent into foreign lands full of danger; they take snapshots of random places and then make general—critics might say wild—statements about the world at large. They play a high-stakes game, ever wary of the tyranny of the unknown, ever worried about the consequence of miscalculation. Their special talent is the *educated guess*, with emphasis on the adjective. The leaders of the pack are practical-minded people who rely on detailed observation, directed research, and data analysis. Their Achilles heel is the big *I*, when they let intuition lead them astray.

This chapter celebrates two groups of statistical modelers who have made lasting, positive impacts on our lives. First, we meet the epidemiologists whose investigations explain the causes of disease. Later, we meet credit modelers who mark our fiscal reputation for banks, insurers, landlords, employers, and so on. By observing these scientists in action, we will learn how they have advanced the technical frontier and to what extent we can trust their handiwork.

~ # # # ~

In November 2006, the U.S. Senate Committee on Health, Education, Labor, and Pensions held a public hearing to second-guess the response of the Food and Drug Administration (FDA) to the just-abated *E. coli* outbreak. The atmosphere was surprisingly cordial, as all seven expert witnesses shared one uplifting narrative. They all commended the public-health agencies for pinpointing spinach as the *cause* of the outbreak in record time and for organizing a bold and broad product recall that prevented many more citizens from falling ill.

Only two months earlier, on September 8, officials from Wisconsin had first set the clock ticking by disclosing a suspicious cluster of five cases of *E. coli*–related illnesses. A week later, the FDA persuaded key producers to recall all fresh spinach produce. Within eighteen days, on the strength of incessant sleuthing, investigators retraced the convoluted path from contamination to disease—linking case after case to spinach processed at a three-acre farm in California during a specific shift on a specific day, spinach that would later reach homes as bagged, prewashed Dole baby spinach. The speed and precision of discovery announced another triumph of the modern science of disease detection, also known as *epidemiology*. Consumer groups praised the collaborative effort by scientists and public officials; even the produce industry promptly accepted responsibility. Against this feel-good backdrop, the Senate hearing centered on ways to support the agencies through funds or technology.

But there is more than one way to tell a good story.

Let's rewind and start over.

On August 15, a batch of spinach got contaminated at a producer in California. Ten days later, Marion Graff of Manitowoc, Wisconsin, fell ill after eating spinach from a salad bar. Soon after, she checked into a hospital. She would go on to become Victim Number 1 of the emergent outbreak. In the next few weeks, the tainted spinach found its way to twenty-six states, afflicting at least two hundred people. By September 1, the outbreak reached a peak and started to ebb. Two more weeks passed before the FDA initiated the spinach recall on September 14. By then, new infections had slowed to a trickle. So in all likelihood, the outbreak died a natural death. Indeed, given the short shelf life of spinach, all of the infected batch would have degraded before the recall took shape. In the meantime, mass hysteria summarily crippled nationwide spinach consumption for months, dealing the industry a direct hit of over $100 million in revenues. In the end, three unlucky people perished out of roughly fifty million who eat spinach in any given week.

If you are discomforted by the retold story, you are not alone. While both narratives are factual, the official story is simple comfort food. With scant scrutiny, consumer groups and the media gobbled it up. The retelling is like spicy Buffalo wings, the juicy bits caught inside the hard bones. Was it blind trust we gave to the FDA? How did the new science ascertain cause–effect? How did five sick people turn a nation into panicked consumers? Was there a fine line between protection and overreaction? The alternative narrative exposes these hard, practical facts of life. And it is the kind of story made for this book.

~ # # # ~

Some legislative hearings are less cordial than others; those involving the credit-scoring industry can be downright acrimonious. Since the 1990s, bills restricting the usage of credit scores have become de rigueur on the legislative agendas of at least forty states. The credit score is a three-digit number computed from credit reports, designed to estimate the chance of someone defaulting on a loan. The technology works by analyzing characteristics purported to be positive or negative indicators of such behavior. Every year, consumer groups introduce us to another handful of wronged consumers who express outrage over rejected loans or soaring interest rates, blamed on incorrect or incomprehensible credit scores. The rhetoric is vicious. Texas state representative Steven Wolens voiced a common sentiment most colorfully: "I am opposed to the notion that people who don't pay their bills on time are more likely to have hail damage to their roofs." By this, he challenged the industry to produce evidence of a direct cause–effect relationship between the indicators used in credit scoring and home insurance claims. Other critics deride the technology as "garbage in, credit score out," charging the credit-reporting agencies with gross incompetence in compiling data that form the basis of credit scores. Still others accuse insurers of co-opting credit scoring as "the 21st century tool for redlining," referencing the outlawed commercial practice of denying mortgages to inner-city neighborhoods.

The supporters of credit scoring are equally fervent. At the Federal Reserve, then-chairman Alan Greenspan averred, "Lenders have taken advantage of credit scoring models and other techniques for efficiently extending credit to a broader spectrum of consumers. The widespread adoption of these models has reduced the costs of evaluating the creditworthiness of borrowers, and in competitive markets, cost reductions tend to be passed through to borrowers." First marketed in the United States in the 1960s, credit-scoring technology has commanded powerful validation in the marketplace; by 2000, more than ten billion scores were said to be used annually. Today, it plays an integral role in the approval for credit cards, auto and home loans, small-business loans, insurance policies, apartment rentals, and even employment. The senior vice president of one regional bank raved, "As you analyze the portfolio [of loans], you can see that the scorecards absolutely work," explaining that the bank made thirty-three times as many loans while losses held steady. It is astonishing that this track record hinges entirely on computers identifying repetitive patterns of behavior, often called *correlations*, without recourse to cause–effect. No wonder Tim Muris, former chairman of the Federal Trade Commission (FTC), remarked, "The average American today enjoys access to credit and financial services, shopping choices, and educational resources that earlier Americans could never have imagined."

Each side, bearing its own script, clashes year after year. The populist narrative assails the practice of credit scoring as harmful to consumers, while the alternative extols the far-reaching benefits of the science. How can we determine whether credit scores are helping people or hurting them? What is the logic behind the science? Where is the fine line between protection and overreaction?

It turns out statistics is at the heart of epidemiology as well as credit scoring. These two fields attract the particular breed of statisticians called modelers. Their special talent is the educated guess; their handiwork informs vital decisions in business and public policy. Just as epidemiologists pinpoint the causes of diseases, credit modelers uncover the indicators of undesirable consumer behavior. For their achievements, these statisticians have garnered paltry attention. In this chapter, we shine a light on their craft, beginning with one suburban family in Middle America.

~ # # # ~

On September 7, 2006, doctors at Elmbrook Memorial Hospital in Manitowoc County, Wisconsin, readmitted Lisa Brott after her stool tested positive for *E. coli*, a type of bacteria that can cause discomfort, kidney failure, and even death. Subsequent examination revealed that her blood and kidneys were infected by a virulent class of the bacteria referred to as O157:H7; in the ensuing eight days, Lisa received head-to-toe blood replacement through a slit in her neck. Another resident of Manitowoc, Marion Graff, age seventy-seven, fell ill while taking a bus trip for seniors and later died of *E. coli*–induced kidney failure in a hospital in Green Bay.

Every year, a handful or a dozen Manitowoc residents contract *E. coli*; the infections frequently occur in clusters, especially in the summertime, due to the popularity of water sports and barbecue parties. Most of these illnesses are "sporadic," not linked to an outbreak, and thus cause no special alarm. The presence of incidental cases, however, makes daunting the detection of the beginnings of a true outbreak. As each new case shows up, one must decide if it is part of an upward trend or not. How long does one wait before declaring an outbreak? Between prescience and prevarication is a tight space!

The Manitowoc health office believed they had detected a localized cluster, as four of the five patients attended the county fair in late August and presumably came into contact with livestock, a familiar source of *E. coli*. The five cases were reported to Dr. Jeffrey Davis, the state's chief medical officer for communicable diseases, who had also learned about another *E. coli* cluster in Dane County. Since Wisconsin sees hundreds of *E. coli* cases each year, Dr. Davis's staff was unsure whether this summertime spurt was anything out of the ordinary.

Then, on September 8, the office received word about five patients in five hospitals who had been treated for severe kidney failure in the preceding few days. The educated guess pointed to an outbreak. Later that day, the state laboratory discovered that eight patients had identical strains of O157:H7. Because more than 3,520 such strains have been documented, each with a distinctive "DNA fingerprint," this finding strongly suggested a common source. Dr. Davis determined that a statewide outbreak was under way, and he alerted the Centers for Disease Control and Prevention (CDC) in Atlanta, Georgia.

Meanwhile, disease detectives in Oregon also were hot on the trail after microbiologists confirmed a cluster of three O157:H7 cases on September 8 and a further three cases on September 13. Dr. Bill Keene, the head epidemiologist, recognized a statewide outbreak, and he also notified the CDC.

At the CDC, Molly Joyner managed the database of PulseNet, suggestively described by Dr. Davis as "a dating service for bacteria." Each year, public-health labs around the country contribute over five thousand E. coli fingerprints to this national database. Joyner prescreened the entrants, looking for close matches. On September 11, she noticed Wisconsin's submission of eight related E. coli cases. This strain resembled one previously found in hamburger patties in Texas, and its DNA was indistinguishable from earlier submissions by nine other states. The now-familiar story replayed itself at the federal level. Joyner was used to seeing two or three uploads of O157:H7 in any given week, reaching a seasonal high during the summer. The specific strain had never been linked to any U.S. outbreaks before, but since 1998, it was appearing more and more often. She wondered if all these cases could be connected. When another new case arrived from Minnesota, she pulled the trigger. (Figure 2-1 illustrates the decision facing Joyner every year as cases are reported to the CDC.)

First individual states and then the federal agencies mobilized. A deadly bacterium on the loose was like a ticking time bomb: there was precious little time to locate it and then defuse it. In Wisconsin and Oregon, the disease detectives sprang into action, calling patients and their families to ask about their eating habits. However, the first round of interviews failed to uncover a "smoking gun," that is, the tainted food item eaten by the patients before they fell ill. In Manitowoc, John Brott, Lisa's husband of twenty-seven

Figure 2-1 Between Prescience and Prevarication: The CDC Pulled the Trigger

In 2006, CDC did not declare an outbreak till early September despite a spurt of cases during the summer. (Note: the two charts have different scales.)

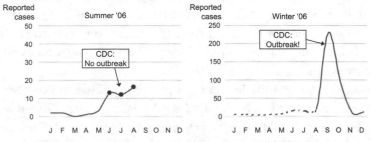

In 2005, a similar spurt of cases occurred in the summer. If CDC had declared an outbreak, it would have been proven incorrect by the winter.

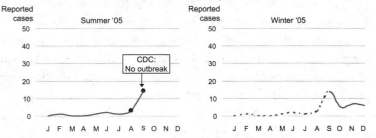

2004 was a year with no outbreaks, but there were incidental cases. The existence of incidental cases is what makes outbreak investigations hard.

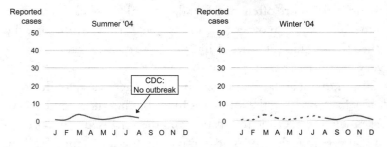

years, told investigators Lisa did not eat red meat, did not drink, and loved green salads, especially in the summer. This report threw them off guard. As the county health officer explained, "Let's say someone went out and had a hamburger and a salad. Almost automatically, you would think the hamburger is the link to *E. coli* because that has been the past history." About 40 percent of past food-borne outbreaks were caused by contaminated beef—not surprising, since cow intestines harbor E. *coli* bacteria.

To be fair, all epidemiological evidence collected during these early stages is conflicting and patchy, half facts and half speculation without an obvious dividing line. Try as they might, patients cannot pinpoint each food injested and every restaurant visited in the recent past, so their answers are bound to be incomplete, inaccurate, or even misleading.

In Oregon, Dr. Keene ordered a much more intrusive questionnaire, nicknamed the "shotgun." To say this survey casts a wide net would be an understatement. Melissa Plantenga, an analyst, spent the night and the next morning peppering five patients with 450 questions each, detailing everything and anything that could have entered their stomachs, including commonplace items like romaine lettuce, eggs, and bottled water, as well as the unusual— such as dried seaweed, cheese from a mail-order source, and homegrown fresh tomatoes from a garden.

It was like trying to find the needle in a haystack, but the reward could prove gratifying: Plantenga would be the first person to propose that "bagged spinach" *caused* this E. *coli* outbreak, and she would later be proven right. She reasoned, "A lot of the time, with [only a few] people, we won't be able to figure the source out. But this time, it seemed odd that I was hearing, 'bagged spinach,' 'bagged spinach.'" Four of her five interviewees mentioned those leafy greens.

Back in Wisconsin, Dr. Davis also ordered more extensive interviews done. The first eight that came back all implicated spinach. In New Mexico, detectives independently suspected leafy greens and collected bags of spinach for lab testing.

So it came hardly as a surprise when Dr. Keene called the CDC about the Oregon outbreak, he found Dr. Davis on the other line. Everything came together: those present recalled, "There was an electrical moment when in the space of one hour, two epidemiological hypotheses matched and the two [DNA] patterns matched." The doctors concluded—thanks to savvy statisticians on the team—that bagged spinach was the cause of an epidemic developing in multiple states.

In only eight days following the first report in Manitowoc, epidemiologists succeeded in detecting the outbreak and determining its scope. It was a marvel how much happened in such a short time. They also deduced its most likely cause. But each passing day brought forth more cases: in Wisconsin, they totaled twenty, with one fatality; in Utah, eleven; in Oregon, five; in Indiana, four; in Michigan, three; in Idaho, three; in New Mexico, two; and in Connecticut, one. The fast-rising case count severely tested the scientists' conviction: if tainted spinach was indeed the cause, then consumers should stop eating the vegetable till the outbreak abated; if it was not the cause, then such an action would devastate an industry while the outbreak would ravage on. The consequence of miscalculation was grave, the stakes high and getting higher.

~ # # # ~

A century and a half ago, a young English doctor found himself in a worse predicament when a string of cholera outbreaks killed tens of thousands between 1830 and 1850. In 1854, around London's Broad Street (now Broadwick Street), 127 people succumbed to the disease in three days, and 500 died in the first ten days. At the time, the cause of cholera was popularly believed to be "miasma," also known as foul air. In a series of inspired studies, Dr. John Snow demonstrated that cholera is spread by foul water, not foul air. By mapping sites of water pumps and homes of the deceased, he guessed correctly that the Broad Street pump was infected. Folklore had it that the outbreak halted as soon as the handle was taken off the pump. (Epidemiologists now believe that other factors such as the flight of residents from the sullied area also contributed to ending the crisis.)

Dr. Snow's epic field investigations marked the beginning of epidemiology of infectious diseases. It was Dr. Alexander Langmuir who brought this discipline to the United States. As CDC's chief epidemiologist, Langmuir in 1951 inaugurated the Epidemic Intelligence Service (EIS), a training program for disease detectives. He conceived and sold the program as a form of "civil defense" against the threat of biological weapons during the Cold War. EIS officers have played leading roles in preventing and controlling diseases, including polio, lead poisoning, Legionnaires' disease, and toxic shock syndrome. They proudly wear lapel pins of a shoe with a hole, symbolizing the sweat and toil involved in their surveillance activities.

In Langmuir's office hung the portraits of his three heroes: John Snow (of course), Sir Edwin Chadwick, and Charles Chapin. Chadwick, like Snow, was instrumental in jump-starting sanitation reform in England in the nineteenth century; he advocated the then-novel concept of using pipes to carry water into residences. Chapin, who served as the health officer of Providence, Rhode Island, for forty-eight years, earning the nickname "the dean of city health officers," ignited the public-health movement in the United States in the 1880s, and he also championed the use of scientific principles.

Langmuir preached the value of collaboration and encouraged people from psychology, anthropology, sociology, and other disciplines to attend EIS training. To date, the program has graduated over three thousand officers, and about 30 percent of those in recent classes are not doctors. EIS officers are celebrated for their balance of analytical rigor and practical outlook.

~ ᚎ ᚎ ᚎ ~

On September 14, the FDA went all-in: announcing the multistate outbreak, it urged consumers not to eat bagged spinach, soon expanded to all fresh spinach. The breadth of the advisory was unprecedented for a vegetable or fruit. But the industry absorbed the shock surprisingly well, and several key players agreed to a sweeping product recall. Restaurants including McDonald's and Subway quickly dropped spinach from their menus. Grocers including Wal-Mart and Safeway yanked spinach off their shelves and salad bars. The media exploded with front-page stories. People dumped what spinach they had at home. For the next five days, U.S. spinach sales evaporated.

Robert Rolfs, the Utah state epidemiologist and an EIS graduate, summarized the rationale well: "Until we get to the bottom of this [outbreak] and find out how widespread it is, what brand it is, where the contamination is, for the short term, I'd suggest people not eat raw spinach." Tacitly, he acknowledged the scientists knew less than what they did not know.

Let's review the evidence up to September 14. Eight states had reported fifty cases. Most of these infections were related because they shared the same strain of O157:H7, the same one out of at least 3,520 known strains in nature. The scientists assumed same strain, same source. Epidemiologists suspected the common source to be tainted spinach on the strength of circumstantial evidence collected through field interviews. No smoking gun had yet been found. The Dole brand was deemed the most likely suspect, but other brands had not been ruled out.

In the meantime, the detectives and scientists were scrambling to beat the clock. The detectives rummaged through kitchens for any leftover bags of spinach, from which the lab technicians attempted to culture E. coli bacteria. Unrelentingly, the case count continued to rise, day after day for six days:

September 15: 95 cases, 19 states
September 16: 102 cases, 19 states
September 17: 109 cases, 19 states
September 18: 114 cases, 21 states

September 19: 131 cases, 23 states
September 20: 146 cases, 23 states

On the seventh day, the big gamble paid off. The New Mexico lab successfully coaxed *E. coli* from leftover spinach to grow, and its fingerprint matched the outbreak strain. Eventually, thirteen of forty-four bags collected from households, all marketed as Dole baby spinach, were found to contain O157:H7, and all thirteen matched the outbreak strain. Thus, the circle was complete.

This auspicious news gave a boost to agricultural inspectors, who had been scouring spinach fields since September 14, looking for clues. From the start, they had suspected California because the Golden State supplies three-quarters of U.S. spinach, and its leafy-greens farms had caused multiple outbreaks in the past; based on interviews, they narrowed their focus to nine ranches. These early efforts were frustrated, as the environmental samples all tested negative for O157:H7. Perhaps the inspectors arrived too late, after the source of contamination had already dissipated. But now the New Mexico lab handed them a bonus gift, in the form of the lot code P227A, retrieved from the packaging of leftover spinach: "P" for the South facility, "227" for the production date of August 15, and "A" for shift A. (Eventually, twelve other bags of spinach were found to have been tainted, and all carried the inauspicious code, except two with missing packaging.) P227A led inspectors to four specific fields. On one of these fields—a three-acre plot leased by Mission Organics in San Benito Valley—and not on the others, inspectors matched the outbreak strain in samples of river water and animal feces.

As the bagged-spinach theory gained traction and new cases ceased to appear, the hardy investigators were finally able to declare victory in what turned out to be a thirty-nine-day war, well fought with unyielding determination and tight teamwork. Indeed, consumer groups became the investigators' greatest cheer-leaders, and the media their obedient messengers. The Senate committee affirmed its goodwill. Seen in this light, the investigation was an utter triumph of the modern science of epidemiology. In the opinion of Caroline Smith DeWaal at the Center for Science in the Public Interest, "Early [action] is good," because the spinach recall prevented "hundreds more cases."

But the lack of scrutiny by consumer groups, particularly in the early stages, appeared misguided after the FDA issued its final report of March 2007. Contrary to DeWaal's assertion, we do not know how many lives—*if any*—were saved by the recall. As always, the true onset of disease preceded the time when patients checked into hospitals or when cases were reported; the earliest known infection occurred on August 19, with 80 percent of the cases reported by September 4, which was ten days before the FDA went all-in. Since the contamination evidently affected a single production run, and since spinach is highly perishable, this outbreak would clearly have wilted on its own. More significantly, to measure the real impact of the recall would require knowing what would have happened had the recall not been instituted. That alternative world of no recall, unfortunately, could only exist in our imagination. So it was impossible, in practice, to prove DeWaal's claim of many lives saved. The same kind of conundrum was recognized over a century ago by John Snow, who considered the possibility that "the [cholera] attacks had so far diminished before the use of the water was stopped that it was impossible to decide whether the well still contained the cholera poison in an active state or whether, from some cause, the water had become free from it." Such inability to gauge the effect of public policy served to raise the stakes further, especially when it has costly side effects.

If few lives could have been saved, then the final toll for this outbreak amounted to three deaths and about a hundred hospitalizations. While the perceived benefit of the recall could not be ascertained, its destruction overnight of an industry with sales of $300 million a year was broadly felt. It took six months for spinach sales to recover by half. The recall also caused collateral damage

as sales of bagged salads without spinach slipped by 5 to 10 percent. Innocents, like smaller farms on the East Coast, especially
suffered. The initial FDA advisory covered the whole country;
subsequent restriction to California provided scarce relief because
shoppers simply could not tell where spinach was grown.

Consumer groups say it is better to be safe than sorry. Before
you agree, take a look at the following list of foods:

Basil	Orange juice
Cabbage	Raspberries
Green onions	Chicken
Lettuce	Ground beef
Parsley	Shellfish
Snow peas	Eggs
Squashes	Milk
Tomatoes	Ice cream
Cantaloupes	Almonds
Green grapes	Peanut butter
Mangoes	Mayonnaise
Melons	Water

Every one of these items has been linked to outbreaks (we are
not even talking about sporadic cases). Over 73,000 Americans
contract O157:H7 each year. If the FDA went all-in every time,
there would not be much food left on the dining table! Expressing
his concern about overzealous regulators, John Baillie, a Salinas
farmer not implicated in this epidemic, sighed, "You can't just say,
'Well, let's throw a dart and see what we hit'; that's just unfair."

Furthermore, it was later determined that simultaneous outbreaks were occurring in Manitowoc. Of the initial cluster of
five cases, tainted spinach caused but one, and the other four,
not matching the outbreak strain, were linked to exposure at the
county fair. A skeptic would argue that the spinach recall turned
five sick patients in Wisconsin into a nation of panicked consum-

ers, that it reflected more overreaction than consumer protection. Did we give blind trust to the FDA and the CDC? Is there a scientific foundation upon which the agencies ascertain cause–effect?

Epidemiology is a fast-moving field that employs statistical modelers who solve real-life puzzles. These modelers specialize in linking causes and effects: they know something happened; they want to know why and how. This task is much more difficult than it seems. *People got sick. They ate spinach. Therefore, spinach made them sick.* Read that again. There is no reason why the last statement need follow from the first two. What if they also ate lettuce? Could lettuce rather than spinach have made them sick? Worse, could lettuce and spinach have combined to make them sick? (Even worse, could they have eaten spinach after they got sick for whatever reason?) The fact that those first two statements could simultaneously be true *and* unrelated makes cause-finding a treacherous enterprise. There are few true paths, perhaps only one, but countless wrong turns.

Such is the confusing landscape these disease detectives have to negotiate. They do not get to choose. Finding causes of diseases is the be-all and end-all in their line of work. Nothing less can be accepted, because the consequence of miscalculation is devastating to the economy and consumer confidence. As we saw, the case count mounted each day the smoking gun was not found. If the investigators were unlucky and were chasing after bad leads, then the delays in identifying the source could be lethal. In this case, it wasn't until spinach was confirmed as the cause of the outbreak that they could utter a sigh of relief.

As statisticians, epidemiologists have evolved a keen sense of the limits of statistics. This is not to say they doubt its power, only that they are smart enough to look for corroborative evidence from microbiologists, agriculture inspectors, patients, and many other sources beyond statistics. "Not invented here" is not a barrier to progress. Since the 1990s, the discovery of lab techniques for matching DNA fingerprints has buttressed field evidence linking tainted foodstuff to infected stool. The labs uncovered a convoluted audit trail stretching from the Mission Organics field in California to households littered across the nation by tracing the *E. coli* strain from water and feces to spinach leaves to stool samples. When Melissa Plantenga picked spinach out of 450 candidates after conducting hours of in-depth interviews with patients, it was only a hunch based on statistics, even if a strong one. The accumulation of evidence from multiple sources clinched her case. Similarly, investigators confirmed the onset date of August 19 in two ways: from epidemiological finding, they realized that no patients who fell sick before this date remembered consuming fresh bagged spinach, and from the lab results, they noted that no *E. coli* DNA from clinical samples collected before this date matched the outbreak strain. Epidemiology generates educated guesses; lab work tests their plausibility.

The core role of statistical thinking should not be underestimated. Consider the indispensable role played by the CDC's information-sharing networks in the spinach outbreak investigation. PulseNet links together public-health laboratories and maintains a national database of DNA fingerprints of food-borne pathogens. OutbreakNet connects epidemiologists who share local tidbits and learning. FoodNet, comprising the state health departments, compiles statistics on general trends, such as food exposure rates. This infrastructure, created in the 1990s, has enabled disease detectives to gain strength in numbers by combining observations from multiple local sites. The modern science of networks elegantly overcomes the extremely daunting challenge of scarce information, particularly at the onset of an outbreak, when there may be as few as one patient, and when local news has yet to spread. As John Besser, a lab manager from Minnesota, explained, "PulseNet has been the biggest breakthrough by increasing the specificity of the case definitions. We can now see the connections you would not have seen before, which has revolutionized the world of food safety." Recall the electrifying moment when officials from Oregon and Wisconsin matched their hypotheses during a conference call with the CDC.

The most striking innovation is the *case–control study*. The "controls" draw a baseline against which the "cases" can be judged. In our example, the cases were the *E. coli* patients; the controls were a sampling of people who were not infected but were otherwise comparable in every conceivable way, such as having similar age, income, and ethnicity. Through interviews, Oregon found that four out of five cases ate bagged spinach. This 80 percent figure must be judged in the proper context. If 20 percent of the controls also ate spinach, it would be highly suggestive, but if 80 percent of the controls also ate spinach, it would appear unremarkable. A statistic like that is the difference between a little thing and nothing at all. For this reason, problems with less popular foods, like raw oysters, are easier to catch than those with common foods. More sophisticated researchers use *matched* controls: the control group is recruited from the uninfected to match the characteristics of the infected. Since 70 percent of the spinach *E. coli* cases afflicted women, investigators would replicate this gender imbalance when recruiting controls for interviews.

Interestingly, our spinach detectives took a shortcut. Instead of interviewing any controls, they used the entire Oregon population. (This was all right because the point of controls was to establish a reference level.) For this trick, they were indebted to the foresight of FoodNet, which had conducted large-scale surveys measuring the proportions of Americans eating different foods on a regular basis. According to the FoodNet atlas of exposures, one in five Oregonians eat spinach in any given week. Put next to this number, the 80 percent rate of exposure to spinach among the infected cases looked extraordinary. With a bit of statistics, Dr. Keene made sense of the scale of this difference. If his staff had interviewed five people chosen at random, one of them would be expected to mention bagged spinach to Plantenga. The probability of getting four out of five was below 1 percent. And there they had the origin of the spinach hypothesis.

The case–control study was invented in the 1950s by Sir Bradford Hill and his associates to prove that cigarette smoking causes lung cancer. Hill was also famous for nine "viewpoints" on cause and effect, which continue to affect epidemiological thinking today. By my count, the spinach investigation satisfied six of the nine points:

Hill's Nine Viewpoints

Used	Not Used
1. Strong association	5. Higher dose, stronger response
2. Consistent across people, geography, time	8. Experimental evidence
	9. Analogy
3. Specific: one cause, one effect	
4. Cause precedes effect	
6. Biologically plausible	
7. Coherent with past knowledge	

Following Hill, generations of epidemiologists acknowledge that without a monstrous and meticulous effort, any assertion of cause–effect is tenuous. Because no statistical model can capture the truth in nature, these statisticians strive toward a more modest goal: to create useful models for understanding and controlling diseases. In this regard, they have triumphed. The *New England Journal of Medicine* celebrated "application of statistics" as one of the most important developments in medicine in the twentieth century, amidst obligatory selections involving anatomy, cells, anesthesia, genetics, and so on. Indeed, the invention of the case–control study, the aggregation of scarce information via networks, and the integration of statistical, laboratory, and field findings have contributed mightily to the success of outbreak investigations. Even though these statisticians admit that models are always "wrong" insofar as they represent only educated guesses, they are certain that what they do benefits society. They are able to see the virtue of being wrong.

~ # # # ~

The vital achievements of statisticians working in epidemiology impress us more if we recognize the challenges they face every day:

- Minimal data (Judgments hinge on fewer than ten cases.)
- Urgency (People are dying.)
- Incomplete information (Some say, "I don't recall.")
- Unreliable information (People could imagine things.)
- Necessity to find cause (This pursuit opens up many ways to err.)
- Consequence of mistakes (This one is self-explanatory.)

Their world is not the norm. Other statisticians enjoy more forgiving circumstances:

- Massive data (They analyze millions of cases, literally.)
- Sufficient time (Conclusions are repeatedly tested and refined.)
- Interest in patterns only (They hardly care about cause.)
- Lower stakes (No one dies.)

Blessed with these favors, credit modelers feel confident that they stand on firmer ground than the disease detectives. Consequently, they experience a rude awakening when they find their work vigorously scorned and their profession endlessly attacked by the same consumer groups that embrace epidemiology. Their story is next.

~ # # # ~

On a day like any other day, Barbara Ritchie drove her three sons to soccer practice in her dependable Toyota minivan. While the kids dashed around the field, she rang up GEICO to ask about the multicar discount on their automotive insurance, as her husband, George, was in the market for a new sedan. After practice, with the boys screaming at each other in the back seats, Barbara stopped next at Blockbuster to pick up some Disney videos. She put the tab on her Visa, making a mental note to pay the credit card bill on time. Then, they joined the crowd at Costco to stock up for the new school year. She used her brand-new American Express card, quietly content that the 4.99 percent introductory APR would cut their interest payments in half. Late in the afternoon, she arrived back at their split-level house. Logging on to the soccer team's website, she ordered kits for the upcoming season. Nearly all the other kids had switched to the new style, so she could not hold out anymore, even if they cost a small fortune. Why not spread the burden over six months with the new credit card?

The Ritchies represent one slice of Americans, imaginatively named "Kids and Cul-de-Sacs" by Claritas, a marketing research company. This demographic segment rose to national prominence in the late 1990s via the political catchphrase "soccer moms," the awe-inspiring stay-at-home mothers who run their households with precision and raise the kids with undivided dedication. Only a few decades ago, Barbara's lifestyle was unheard of. Do you know why the Toyota dealer let her drive the $30,000 minivan off the lot without leaving any of her cash? (Surely, he worried that she could cross state lines and disappear.) How about why GEICO would conduct business strictly over the phone? (Surely, they at least wanted to meet Barbara and George to make sure they are sane drivers.) Their mortgage company had approved their online request for a thirty-year, $400,000 loan in mere minutes. Wonder why? (Without the mortgage, the Ritchies would almost certainly have moved into a more modest home.) Costco "preapproved" Barbara for a credit card without her expressing interest. Can you guess how that happened? (Without the store card, her kids would surely have had to wear their old soccer kits for one more season.) These conveniences are products of what Tim Muris, former FTC chairman, has dubbed "the miracle of instant credit": in America today, a lot of us can borrow money in an instant, without intrusive interviews or character references, without money down, without collateral. Consumer credit has evolved from a privilege to a right. It seems as if some eager lender is around the corner just in case we want to spend money. It has not always been this way, and it still is not in most other countries, even highly industrialized ones.

As Muris elaborated, "This 'miracle' [of instant credit] is only possible because of our credit reporting system." It is not exaggerating much to say that our financial well-being hinges on a number between 300 and 850. This numeral, popularly called the "credit score," is a summary of the credit report, which contains details of our borrowing and payment history, such as how much money we have borrowed, how much we have paid back, whether our loans have been in arrears, what types of loans we possess, and so on. These three digits pack a powerful punch. Mortgage companies, credit card companies, auto and home insurers, other lenders, and even landlords, employers, and cell-phone providers rely on credit scores to handpick customers, set prices, or both.

FICO, the firm that invented credit scoring in the 1960s, has grown from humble beginnings into an $825 million company. Lenders were the first to jump on board. Even in the best of times, some portion of their customers will default for any number of reasons, such as negligence, financial difficulty, and fraud. Too many people stop sending in payments, and the lender goes bust. If every customer has an equal chance of default, lending is just gambling; what makes it a different business is that some borrowers pose better "risks" than others. The successful lender exploits this market structure by demanding higher interest from bad risks or by avoiding them altogether. This sounds too easy, so what is the catch? It is too late to recognize the bad risks after one has already forked over the cash, so lenders must stop less "creditworthy" customers at the door. Like disease detectives, lenders must master the educated guess.

Before FICO changed the game, the decision to grant credit was a craft, passed from master to apprentice: get to know the applicant's *character*, assess his *capacity* to repay the debt, determine *collateral* to secure the loan. The secrets of this business were heavily guarded rules of thumb. Each rule concerned a characteristic known to reflect creditworthiness or lack thereof. Having held a job for many years was regarded as a favorable trait, while renters were considered less desirable than homeowners. Examining an applicant's file, credit officers judged whether the borrower was a good risk on the balance of positive and negative characteristics. These guidelines are best visualized as if–then statements:

IF   the applicant is a painter, plumber, or paperhanger
THEN   reject

IF   the applicant has ever been bankrupt
THEN   reject

IF   the applicant's total debt payment exceeds
            36 percent of income
THEN   reject

Over time, each lender carefully conceived and refined a set of rules. They required that the past foretell the future. The lender who had suffered losses from several painter-borrowers in the past assumed that other painters would behave likewise. While imperfect, such guidelines survived the passage of time and benefited from accumulated wisdom. Like vintage wine, they improved with age. Perfection was out of bounds insofar as human behavior is complicated. No two people were completely synched, and worse, the same person could act differently on two occasions. Therefore, some accepted loans inevitably went unpaid, while some rejected applicants turned up at competitors and became their prized customers. At year's end, credit officers were evaluated by the proportion of accepted loans that had gone bad. This policy encouraged them to accept only clear winners, turning down any borderline cases. By extending less credit only to the most worthy, they ensured that consumer credit remained tight before the advent of scoring. In 1960, only 7 percent of U.S. households held a credit card, and over 70 percent of bank loans were secured by collateral.

Then, in the 1960s, one of the most exciting practical applications of statistical modeling debuted. As conceived by Bill Fair and Earl Isaac, the FICO credit score predicts the chance of a borrower to default on his loan during the subsequent two years. A higher FICO indicates a smaller chance of missing a payment. Although complex, the FICO formulas were well suited for modern computers, so the adoption of credit scores also heralded the era of automated underwriting. Easy online applications and near-instant approval of unsecured consumer loans were both fruits of these developments. Eventually, credit-scoring technology swept the lending industry by storm. How did it work, and what made it so successful?

Statistical scoring algorithms are nothing more than computer programs that harvest enormous collections of complicated rules. (They could not be anything more, because they are conceived by human beings. As of today, "artificial intelligence," the dream of superhuman thinking machines, has yet to honor the hype.) Compared with traditional underwriting, credit scoring is faster, broader, better, and cheaper. A "complicated" rule might look like this:

IF	Years on Job = 2.5 to 5.5
AND	Occupation = Retired
AND	Rent or Own = Rent
AND	Years at Address = 0 to 0.5
AND	Have Major Credit Card = Yes
AND	Banking Relationship = No Information
AND	Number of Recent Credit Inquiries = 1
AND	Account Balances = 16 to 30 percent of Credit Lines
AND	Past Delinquency = None
THEN	Score = 720

This one rule contains nine characteristics. For each applicant, the computer calculates the nine values from information found in his application form and credit report; any applicant fitting this rule receives a score of 720. Say a second applicant resembles him, except that she has a savings account and five recent credit inquiries. She gets scored 660 according to a different but related rule:

IF	Years on Job = 2.5 to 5.5
AND	Occupation = Retired
AND	Rent or Own = Rent
AND	Years at Address = 0 to 0.5
AND	Have Major Credit Card = Yes
AND	Banking Relationship = **Savings**
AND	Number of Recent Credit Inquiries = **5**
AND	Account Balances = 16 to 30 percent of Credit Lines
AND	Past Delinquency = None
THEN	Score = 660

Now imagine thousands upon thousands of such rules, each matching a borrower to a three-digit number. More precisely, this number is a rating of applicants in the past who share similar characteristics as the present borrower. The FICO score is one such system. FICO modelers use 100 characteristics, grouped into five broad categories, listed here in order of importance:

1. Has the applicant dealt responsibly with past and current loans?
2. How much debt is currently held?
3. How long is the credit history?
4. How eagerly is the applicant seeking new loans?
5. Does the applicant have credit cards, mortgages, department store cards, or other types of debt?

In general, whether a score exceeds some cutoff level is far more telling than any individual score. Given a cutoff of 700, Mr. 720 is accepted, while Ms. 660 is rejected. Lenders set cutoff scores so that some desired proportion of applicants will be approved. They believe this proportion represents a healthy mix of good and bad risks needed to keep the business afloat.

The computer-harvested rules outperform the handcrafted ones: covering more details, they facilitate more nuanced comparisons, leading to more accurate predictions. For instance, rather than banning all painters, credit-scoring models selectively grant credit to painters based on other favorable traits. There is a low limit to how many characteristics the human mind can juggle, but the computer has the charming habit of digesting everything it is fed. Moreover, under each characteristic, the computer typically places applicants into five to ten groups, while traditional rules use only two. So instead of using debt ratio above or below 36 percent, a computer rule might split borrowers into groups of High (more than 50 percent), Medium (15 to 35 percent), Low (1 to 14 percent), and Zero debt ratio. This extra complexity achieves the same effect as gerrymandering does in creating voter districts. In the United States, the major political parties realize that simple rules based on things like county lines do not round up as many like-minded voters as do meandering boundaries. The new guidelines can appear illogical, but their impact is undeniable.

Automated scoring also has the advantage of being consistent. In the past, different companies, or analysts within the same company, frequently applied different rules of thumb to the same type of applicants, so credit decisions appeared confused and at times contradictory. By contrast, credit-scoring modelers predetermine a set of characteristics upon which all borrowers are evaluated so that no one characteristic dominates the equation. The computer then gives each applicant a rating, taking into account the importance of each characteristic. In the past, analysts weighed relative importance on the fly at their discretion; these days, FICO computers scan large databases to determine the most accurate weights. In these respects, credit scoring is fair.

It used to take generations to calibrate a simple rule such as "Don't lend to painters"; computers can do the job in less than a second because they excel at repetitive tasks like trial and error. This extreme efficiency lends itself to discovering, monitoring, and refining thousands, even millions, of rules. Moreover, computers allow lenders to track the result of each loan decision, rather than knowing only the overall performance of an entire portfolio, thereby facilitating a more surgical diagnosis of why some decisions turned sour. The feedback loop is much shorter, so weaker rules get eliminated fast.

Early adopters reaped immediate and dramatic gains from statistical scoring systems. An experienced loan officer took about twelve and half hours to process an application for a small-business loan; in the same amount of time, a computer scored fifty applications. In this world, it is hardly surprising that Barbara Ritchie took out an auto loan with so little hassle—over 80 percent of auto loan approvals occur within an hour, and almost a quarter are approved within ten minutes. In this world, it is no wonder Barbara Ritchie was handed a Costco credit card—store clerks can open new accounts in less than two minutes. Thanks to credit scoring, the cost to process card applications has dropped by 90 percent, and the cost to originate a mortgage has been halved.

Lenders have reacted by ratcheting throughput up 25 percent, approving a great many more loans. As a result, the arrival of credit-scoring technology coincided with an explosion of consumer credit. In 2005, American households borrowed $2.1 trillion, excluding mortgages, a sixfold jump in twenty-five years. In turn, this spurred consumer consumption as credit empowered Americans to spend future income on current wants. Today, household expenditures account for two-thirds of the American economy; it is widely believed that heady consumers pulled the United States out of the 2001 recession. Amazingly, higher throughput did not erode quality: the loss rate of new loans turned out to be lower than or equal to the existing portfolio, just as the modelers prescribed. Further, all socioeconomic strata shared the bonanza: among households with income in the bottom 10 percent, the use of credit cards leaped almost twentyfold, from 2 percent in 1970 to 38 percent in 2001; among African-American households, it more than doubled from 24 percent in 1983 to 56 percent in 2001.

Before credit card companies fully embraced credit scores in the 1980s, they targeted only the well-to-dos; by 2002, each household had on average ten credit cards, supporting $1.6 trillion of purchases and $750 million of borrowing. During the 1990s, insurers jumped on board, followed by mortgage lenders. As of 2002, providers of substantially all credit cards, 90 percent of auto loans, 90 percent of personal loans, and 70 percent of mortgages utilized credit scores in the approval process. In industry after industry, it appears that, once let in the door, credit scoring is here to stay. What makes it so sticky?

Credit-scoring models rate the creditworthiness of applicants, allowing users to separate good risks from bad. This ability to select customers, balancing good and bad risks, is crucial to many industries. The insurance industry is no exception. People who tend to file more claims—say, reckless drivers—are more likely to want to buy insurance because they know those who do not file claims in effect subsidize those who do. If an insurer takes in too many bad risks, then the good customers will flee, and the business will falter. In the 1990s, insurance companies realized that credit scores could help them manage risk. To understand how this technology got to dominate industries, let's divide the players into Haves (those who use scoring) and Have-Nots. Thanks to scoring, the first Have cherry-picks the good risks with efficiency. The riskier borrowers are turned away, and they line up behind the Have-Nots. Before long, the Have-Nots notice deterioration in their loss performance. The most discerning Have-Not figures out why; it implements scoring to even the playing field, thus becoming a Have. As more and more firms turn into Haves, the Have-Nots see ever-worsening results, and eventually everyone converts. Acknowledging this domino effect, Alan Greenspan once remarked:

> *"Credit-scoring technologies have served as the foundation for the development of our national markets for consumer and mortgage credit, allowing lenders to build highly diversified loan portfolios that substantially mitigate credit risk. Their use also has expanded well beyond their original purpose of assessing credit risk. Today they are used for assessing the risk-adjusted profitability of account relationships, for establishing the initial and ongoing credit limits available to borrowers, and for assisting in a range of activities in loan servicing, including fraud detection, delinquency intervention, and loss mitiga-*

*tion. These diverse applications have played a major role in pro-
moting the efficiency and expanding the scope of our credit-delivery
systems and allowing lenders to broaden the populations they are
willing and able to serve profitably."*

But this story can also be told in an alternative version.

To hear it from consumer advocacy groups, credit scoring is a
wolf in sheep's clothing: its diffusion is a national tragedy, the science behind it fatally flawed. Birny Birnbaum, at the Center for
Economic Justice, has warned that credit scoring will bring about
the "end of insurance." Chi Chi Wu of the National Consumer
Law Center has charged that credit scoring is "costing consumers billions and perpetuating the economic racial divide." Norma
Garcia, speaking for the Consumers Union, has declared, "Consumers [are] caught in the crossfire." Such was the torrent of dis-
approval that *Contingencies*, an actuarial trade publication, gave
advice on adjusting to "living without credit scoring." Owing to
the unrelenting pressure by consumer groups, at least forty states
as of 2004 have passed laws constraining the use of credit scoring.
Some states, including California, Maryland, and Hawaii, have
barred home and auto insurers from applying the technology. The
FTC amended the Fair Credit Reporting Act in 1996 and again in
2003. Not a year passes without some legislature holding hearings
on the subject. These meetings are like a traveling circus with four
acts; the same four basic themes are repeated over and over and
over again:

1. Ban or heavily censor credit scoring because the statistical
   models are flawed. The models fail to link cause and effect.
   Worse, they unfairly slap minorities and low-income
   households with lower scores.
2. Ban or heavily censor credit scoring until credit reports
   contain accurate and complete information on every

consumer. Data problems are causing many consumers to pay higher rates for loans and insurance.

3. Require credit-scoring companies to open the "black boxes" that hold the proprietary scoring rules. Consumers have a right to inspect, challenge, and repair their credit scores.

4. Conduct more studies or hearings to seek the perfect model of consumer behavior. This research should focus on establishing cause—effect or on measuring disparate impact on the underprivileged.

Many a critique of credit scoring begins and ends with the horror story of a wronged consumer. James White became one in 2004 after his insurer hiked his rate by 60 percent. He learned that his credit score had been marked down substantially because of twelve recent credit inquiries (this was five times the national average of 2.4). Each inquiry occurred when someone requested his credit report, and White was shopping for a mortgage, an auto loan, and a credit card at the time. Critics complained that lenders inspecting his credit report could not have *caused* a change in White's creditworthiness, so it was nonsensical for modelers to relate the two. Extending this line of thought, they contended that scoring models should employ only characteristics that have a proven causal relationship with failure to repay loans. To them, predicting the behavior of people is analogous to explaining the origin of diseases.

In response, credit modelers maintain that they have never sought to find cause; their models find personal traits that are strongly *correlated* with the behavior of defaulting on loans. Correlation describes the tendency of two things moving together, in the same or opposite directions. In James White's case, the model observed that, historically, borrowers who experienced a spurt of credit inquiries were much more likely to miss payments compared with those who did not. Most probably, neither thing directly affected the other.

Indeed, acting on correlation is vital to our everyday experience. Imagine that John, who is trudging through snow five steps ahead of you, slips while turning the corner. Then David, Mary, and Peter slip, too. Slickly veering left, you stay upright. You could have tried to find the black ice, linking effect to cause, but you do not. You presume that walking straight would mean slipping. You act on this correlation. It saves you from the fall. Similarly, when it feels murky outside, you bring an umbrella. You don't study meteorology. Before you move your family to a "good school district," you ask to see standardized test scores. You don't examine whether good schools hire better teachers or just admit smarter students.

How does one live without correlational models? If you think about it, the computer acts like credit officers from yesteryear. If they had noticed the correlation between credit inquiries and failure to pay, they would have used it to disqualify loan applicants, too.

Not only is causation unnecessary for this type of decision, but it is also unattainable. No physical or biological laws govern human behavior exactly. Humans by nature are moody, petulant, haphazard, and adaptive. Statisticians build models to get close to the truth but admit that no system can be perfect, not even causal models. Sometimes, they see things that are not there, and, to borrow language from mutual-fund prospectuses, past performance may not be repeated. To the relief of their creators, credit-scoring models have withstood decades of real-world testing. The correlations that define these models persist, and our confidence in them grows by the day.

Another common grievance concerns the credit reports, which are known to be inaccurate and often incomplete. Common errors include typing mistakes, mistaken identities, identity fraud, duplicated entries, outdated records, and missing information. Critics say because garbage in must equal garbage out, when "dirty" data are fed to computers, the necessary outcome must be unreliable credit scores.

Nobody disputes the messy state of data hygiene; it is fantasy, however, to assume that any credit-reporting system can be free of error. Between them, the three dominant U.S. credit bureaus process 13 billion data per month; on that base, an error rate as low as 0.01 percent still means one mistake appears every two minutes! Welcome to the real world of massive data. Modelers have developed some powerful strategies to cope. We already observed that each computer rule contains multiple characteristics, and these are often partially redundant. For example, many scoring systems evaluate "years at current residence" together with "years at current job" and "length of credit history." For most people, these three traits are correlated. If one of the triad is omitted or inaccurate, the presence of the other two attenuates the impact. (Sure, a different rule applies, but the score shifts only slightly.) By contrast, credit officers cannot correct course, because their handcrafted rules take one characteristic at a time.

Does inaccurate or incomplete information always harm consumers? Not necessarily: when mistakes happen, some people will receive artificially lower scores, while others will get undeservedly higher scores. For example, the credit bureau could have confused James White's neighbor, a certain Joe Brown, with a namesake New York corporate lawyer, and so attached the latter's stellar debt repayment record to the former's credit report, bumping up his credit score and qualifying him for lower interest rates. For good reason, we never hear about these cases.

Yet another line of attack by the critics of credit-scoring technology asserts the right of consumers to verify and repair their credit scores. This legislative push engendered the Fair and Accurate Credit Transactions Act of 2003. Innocuous as it sounds, this misguided initiative threatens to destroy the miracle of instant credit. In this era of openness, people disgruntled with bad scores have started knocking on the doors of credit repair agencies, hoping for a quick fix. Dozens of shady online brokers have cropped up to help customers piggyback on the good credit records of strangers by becoming "authorized users" on their credit cards. The customers inherit these desirable credit histories, which elevate their credit scores. This is identity theft turned upside down: cardholders with high FICO scores willingly rent out their identities for $125 a pop. The online brokers, who charge $800 per repaired account, act as the eBay-style marketplace for buying and selling creditworthiness! This dubious tactic distorts credit scores, blurring the separation between good and bad risks. Faced with more losses, lenders would eventually have to turn away more applicants or raise rates. In 2007, FICO moved to close the loophole, eliminating the "authorized user" characteristic from its scoring formulas. However, this solution harms legitimate types of authorized users such as young adults leveraging their parents' history or one spouse rehabilitating the other's credit.

Piggybacking is but one example of credit repair scams, which will multiply as more knowledge about credit-scoring algorithms becomes available. In the extreme, unscrupulous credit repair services promise to remove negative but accurate items, and some bombard credit bureaus with frivolous disputes in the hope that creditors will fail to respond within thirty days, after which time such disputed items must be temporarily removed as per the law. The trouble with disclosure, with opening up the "black boxes," is that people with bad scores are more likely to be actively looking for errors, and that only negative items on reports will be challenged or corrected. Over time, the good risks will get lower scores than they deserve because they have not bothered to verify their credit reports, while the bad risks will get higher scores than they deserve because only beneficial errors remain on theirs. Consequently, the difference between bad risks and good risks may vanish along with other positives associated with credit scoring. Such an outcome would harm the majority of law-abiding, creditworthy Americans. There is a real danger that overly aggressive consumer protection efforts will backfire and kill the goose that lays the golden egg.

Much alarming rhetoric has also been spewed over discriminatory practices allegedly hidden in credit-scoring technology. Both sides acknowledge that the underprivileged have a lower *average* credit score than the general population. But income disparity is the economic reality which no amount of research will erase. Credit-scoring models, which typically do not use race, gender, or income characteristics, merely reflect the correlation that poorer people are less likely to have the means to pay back loans. Simple rules of old would have turned down the entire class; that was why credit cards were originally toys for the rich. Credit-scoring models, by virtue of complexity, actually approve some portion of underprivileged applicants. Recall that in the past, certain lenders rejected all painters and plumbers, but computers today accept some of them on account of other positive traits. The statistics bear out this point: from 1989 to 2004, households earning $30,000 or less were able to boost borrowing by 247 percent. Many studies have shown that access to credit has expanded in all socioeconomic strata since credit scoring began. Going backward would only reverse this favorable trend.

In their dogged campaign against credit scoring, consumer groups have achieved mixed results to date. For example, Representative Wolens's bid to ban credit scoring by insurers in Texas was defeated. Similar legislative drives failed in Missouri, Nevada, New York, Oregon, and West Virginia. The strategy to go after the statistical foundation directly has proven unwise, given the solid foundation of the science. Credit-scoring technology is inarguably superior to the old way of underwriting by handcrafted rules of thumb. Having been deployed at scale, it gains affirmation with each passing day.

~###~

In this chapter, we have seen two innovations of statistics that have made tremendous, positive impact on our lives: epidemiology and credit scoring. The breed of statisticians known as the modelers has taken center stage. A *model* is an attempt to describe the unknowable by using that which is known: In disease detection, the model describes the path of infection (for all cases, including the unreported), based on interview responses, historical patterns, and biological evidence. In credit scoring, the model describes the chance of loan default based on personal traits and historical performance.

These two examples represent two modes of statistical modeling; both can work magic, if done carefully. Epidemiology is an application in which finding *cause* is the only meaningful objective. We can all agree that some biological or chemical mechanism probably exists to cause disease. Taking brash action based on correlations alone might result in entire industries being wiped out while the disease continues to spread. Credit scoring, by contrast, relies on *correlations* and nothing more. It is implausible that something as variable as human behavior can be attributed to simple causes; modelers specializing in stock market investment and consumer behavior have also learned similar lessons. Statisticians in these fields have instead relied on accumulated learning from the past.

The standard statistics book grinds to a halt when it comes to the topic of correlation versus causation. As readers, we may feel as if the authors have taken us along for the ride! After having plodded through the mathematics of regression modeling, we reach a section that screams, "Correlation is not causation!" and, "Beware of spurious correlations!" over and over. The bottom line, the writers tell us, is that almost nothing we have studied can prove causation; their motley techniques measure only correlation. The greatest statistician of his generation, Sir Ronald Fisher, famously scoffed at Hill's technique to link cigarette smoking and lung cancer; he offered that the discovery of a gene that predisposes people to both smoking and cancer would discredit such a link. (This gene has never been found.) In this book, I leave philosophy to the academics (they have been debating the issue for decades). I do not deny that this is a fundamental question. But this is not the way statistics is practiced. Causation is not the only worthwhile goal, and models based on correlations can be very successful. The performance of credit-scoring models has been so uniformly spectacular that one industry after another has fallen in love with them.

George Box, one of our most preeminent industrial statisticians, has observed, "All models are wrong but some are useful." Put bluntly, this means even the best statistical model cannot perfectly represent the real world. Unlike theoretical physicists, who seek universal truths, applied statisticians want to be judged by their impact on society. Box's statement has become a motto to aspiring modelers. They do not care to beat some imaginary perfect system; all they want is to create something better than the status quo. They understand the virtue of being (less) wrong. FICO's scoring technology has no doubt improved upon hand-crafted rules of thumb. The assortment of modern techniques like case–control studies and DNA fingerprint matching advanced the field of epidemiology.

Despite being cut from the same cloth, modelers in these two fields face divergent reception from consumer advocacy groups. Generally speaking, these groups support the work of disease detectives but deeply distrust credit-scoring models. However, epidemiologists face the more daunting task of establishing causation with less data and time, and in that sense, their models are more prone to error. It is clear that a better grasp of the cost and benefit of product recalls will further consumer interest more than yet another study on causality in credit scoring. In the meantime, take heart that modelers are looking out for our health and wealth.

3

Item Bank / Risk Pool

The Dilemma of Being Together

I can define it, but I can't recognize it when I see it.
—LLOYD BOND, EDUCATION SCHOLAR

*Millionaires living in mansions on the water are being
subsidized by grandmothers on fixed incomes in
trailer parks.*
—BOB HARTWIG, INSURANCE INDUSTRY ECONOMIST

The late CEO of Golden Rule Insurance, J. Patrick Rooney,
made his name in the 1990s as the father of the health savings account. For this political cause, he spent $2.2 million of his
own fortune and partnered with conservative icon Newt Gingrich.
For years, he was a generous donor to the Republican Party and a
prominent voice within. In 1996, he ran for governor of Indiana. In
business, he was equally astute, turning Indianapolis-based Golden
Rule into one of the largest marketers of individual health insurance. When Rooney sold his company in 2003 to the industry
giant UnitedHealth Group for half a billion dollars, he delivered a
windfall of about $100,000 to every Golden Rule employee.

Even more than his commercial success, it was Rooney's extra-curricular activities that kept him in the news. He was a maverick before mavericks became fashionable in the Republican set. Given his politics, Rooney was an unlikely defender of civil rights. In the mid-1970s, he noticed that all his insurance agents in Chicago were white—no wonder the firm had struggled to make inroads into the city's key black neighborhoods. He argued persuasively that the licensing examination unfairly disqualified blacks. He sued the developer of the disputed test, Educational Testing Service (ETS), which is better recognized as the company that administers the SAT to millions of high school students in the United States. At the time, test developers adhered to a "don't ask, don't tell" policy when it came to fair testing. The subsequent "Golden Rule settle-ment" between ETS and Rooney pioneered scientific techniques for screening out unfair test questions, defined as those for which white examinees outperformed black examinees by a sizable mar-gin. But statisticians were none too happy about this apparently sensible rule, and the president of ETS publicly regretted his settle-ment. Let's examine why.

~ # # # ~

Even those who did not share Rooney's politics found him endear-ing. He possessed a flair for effortlessly linking his social causes, his profiteering self-interest, and his Christian duty. He made his name as the father of health savings accounts (HSAs), which provide tax benefits to encourage participants to set aside money for medical expenses. Right before Congress authorized HSAs in 2003, a watershed event that owed much to his political savvy and expensive lobbying, Rooney sold his family insurance business to industry giant UnitedHealth Group for $500 million and then created a new business called Medical Savings Insurance (MSI), becoming one of the first in the nation to sell HSAs. Rooney pro-claimed, "I am doing the right thing, and I think the Lord will be pleased about it," satisfied that "when I die, I would like God to welcome me." When asked why MSI made it a habit to underpay hospitals that served his customers, he contended, "We're trying to help the people that are not able to help themselves." In his mind, he was leading the good fight against "shameful" practices of "sinful" executives. The same motives, as much selfless as self-serving, drove him to file the lawsuit against the Illinois Department of Insurance and the Educational Testing Service.

In October 1975, Illinois had launched a new licensing examination for insurance agents, developed by ETS. In short order, it emerged that the passing rate of the new test was merely 31 percent, less than half that of the previous version. In Chicago, one of Rooney's regional managers worried about the supply of black insurance agents needed to reach the 1.2 million blacks in the Windy City. Rooney knew Chicago was a key market for Golden Rule Insurance, so when he got wind of this information, he once again seized the role of a social-justice champion: he charged that "the new test was for all practical purposes excluding blacks entirely from the occupation of insurance agent."

The Illinois Department of Insurance tried to ward off the lawsuit by twice revamping the licensing examination, bringing the passing rate up above 70 percent. But Rooney was a tenacious opponent, and he had an alluring argument. The overall passing rate obscured an unsightly gap between black and white examinees. In the revamped exam, the passing rate of blacks rose in tandem with that of whites, leaving the gap intact. Finally, in 1984, the two sides acceded to the so-called Golden Rule settlement, which required ETS to conduct scientific analysis on tests to ensure fairness.

However one felt about the commercial motivation behind Rooney's lawsuit, it was clear that his confrontational advocacy stimulated some serious rethinking about fair testing. The implications extended well beyond the insurance industry. ETS spearheaded the bulk of this new research, which was to make its strongest impact on college and graduate school admissions tests, as these, after all, supplied the nonprofit test developer and administrator its biggest source of revenue.

~ # # # ~

As admissions to U.S. colleges grow ever more competitive, parents become ever more invested in how their kids perform on admissions tests like the SAT. In Tia O'Brien's neighborhood in Marin County, the lush region just north of San Francisco Bay, boomer parents with college-age children exercise plain old good manners: "Less-than-near-perfect test scores should not be discussed in polite company." Bound for college in 2008, O'Brien's daughter was a member of the biggest class ever to finish high school in California, which has the largest population as well as the most extensive and prestigious public-university system in America. Everywhere she looked, O'Brien saw insanity: anxious parents hired "SWAT teams of test-prep experts," who promised to boost test scores; they paid "stagers" to make over their kids' images; their counselors established "grade-point targets" for various colleges; and "summer-experience advisors" planned activities "every week of the summer," such as community service projects, trips abroad to study languages, and Advanced Placement classes.

These type A parents inadvertently have been nudging the United States out of isolation from the rest of the world. In some European countries and especially in Asia, the shortage of university spots coupled with a long-standing reliance on standardized tests have produced generations of obsessed parents who strive as hard at micromanaging their kids' lives as they do at fulfilling unrealistic expectations. Previously, the United States was an island of serenity in the wild, wide world of university entrance derbies. These days, that is no longer the case.

In Marin, discussing test scores in public is taboo, though we know most students there take the SAT (as do other students in California, where only one in ten college applicants submit scores from the ACT, the other recognized college admissions examination). First administered by ETS in 1926, the SAT was taken by 1.5 million college-bound seniors in 2007; many of them took the test more than once.

The SAT measures a nebulous quantity known as "academic potential"—let's just call it ability—and its advocates point to the strong, proven correlation between SAT scores and eventual college GPA as the technical justification for the exam. Since 2005, each SAT test contains ten sections, three each of reading, mathematics, and writing, plus one "experimental" section. The first section of every test involves essay writing, while the other nine appear in random order. Students are permitted about four hours in which to complete the exam. The sixty-seven items in the reading sections (formerly called verbal) are split between sentence completion (nineteen items) and reading passages (forty-eight). All reading items use the multiple-choice format, requiring students to select the correct answer from five choices. Antonyms and analogies were discontinued in 1994 and 2005, respectively. The three mathematics sections (formerly called quantitative) together contain forty-four multiple-choice items plus ten "grid-in" items requiring direct response, which replaced quantitative comparison items in 2005. Besides the essay, the remaining writing sections consist of multiple-choice items focused on grammar.

Even though the format of each SAT section is fixed, any two students can see different sets of questions, even if they are seated next to each other in the same test center at the same time. This unusual feature acts as a safeguard against cheating but also strikes some of us as an unfair arrangement. What if one version of the test contains more difficult items? Would not one of the two students be disadvantaged? Here is where the "experimental" section comes to the rescue. This special section can measure reading, mathematics, or writing ability and is indistinguishable from the other corresponding sections of the test, but none of its questions count toward the student's total score. This experimental section should properly be considered the playground for psychometricians—statisticians specializing in education. In creating tests, they lift specific items from the scored sections of one version and place them into the experimental section of another. These shared items form a common basis upon which to judge the relative difficulty of the two versions and then to adjust scores as needed.

Statisticians have many other tricks up their sleeves, including how to make tests fair, a topic we shall examine in detail.

~ # # # ~

Asking whether a test item is fair is asking whether it presents the same level of difficulty to comparable groups of examinees. An item is deemed more difficult if a lesser proportion of test takers answers it correctly. Conversely, an easier item has a higher rate of correct answers. Statisticians make tests fair by identifying and removing questions that favor one group over others—say, whites over minorities or males over females. The cure is as simple as it gets. So why did it take almost ten years for Golden Rule and ETS to agree on an operating procedure to address Rooney's complaint about unfair testing? How can something that sounds so simple be so difficult to put into practice?

To explore this issue, let's inspect a set of sample test items, all of which were long-ago candidates for inclusion in SAT verbal sections. The first four are analogy items, and the other two are sentence completion items. See if you can figure out which items proved more difficult for the college-bound students.

1. PLAIT:HAIR
   A. knead:bread
   B. weave:yarn
   C. cut:cloth
   D. fold:paper
   E. frame:picture

2. TROUPE:DANCERS
   A. flock:birds
   B. ferry:passengers
   C. barn:horses
   D. dealership:cars
   E. highway:trucks

3. MONEY:WALLET
   A. rifle:trigger
   B. dart:spear
   C. arrow:quiver
   D. golf:course
   E. football:goalpost

4. DYE:FABRIC
   A thinner:stain
   B. oil:skin
   C. paint:wood
   D. fuel:engine
   E. ink:pen

5. In the past the general had been _____ for
   his emphasis on defensive strategies, but he was _____
   when doctrines emphasizing aggression were discredited.
   A. criticized . . . discharged
   B. parodied . . . ostracized
   C. supported . . . disappointed
   D. spurned . . . vindicated
   E. praised . . . disregarded

6. In order to _____ the health hazard caused by an
   increased pigeon population, officials have added to the
   area's number of peregrine falcons, natural _____ of
   pigeons.
   A. reduce . . . allies
   B. promote . . . rivals

    C. starve . . . prey

    D. counter . . . protectors

    E. lessen . . . predators

Since there were five choices for each question, if all examinees guessed randomly, we would still expect 20 percent to be lucky. Actual test results ranked the items from the hardest to the easiest as follows:

Item 5	17 percent correct (hardest)
Item 1	47 percent correct
Item 3	59 percent correct
Items 2, 6	73 percent correct
Item 4	80 percent correct (easiest)

Notice that the sentence completion item about war strategy (item 5) tripped up so many that the overall correct rate of 17 percent barely departed from the guessing rate. At the other extreme, 80 percent of test takers answered the DYE:FABRIC analogy (item 4) correctly. Comparatively, the MONEY:WALLET analogy (item 3) turned out to be markedly more difficult.

How well did this ranking match your intuition? If there were a few surprises, you would not be alone. Even seasoned analysts have learned that predicting the difficulty level of a test item is easier said than done. No longer teenagers, they are unable to think like teenagers. Moreover, what we just estimated was the overall difficulty for the average test taker; what about which questions put minorities at a disadvantage? In the six sample items, three items were unfair. Can you spot them? (The offending items will be disclosed later.)

It should be obvious by now how hopeless it is to ask human minds to ferret out unfair test questions. At least most of us get to be teenagers once, but alas, a white man would never experience the world of a black female. This was what the eminent scholar of education Lloyd Bond meant when he parodied Justice Potter Stewart's celebrated anti-definition of the obscene: "I could not define it, but I know it when I see it." Bond experiences unfairness as something he can define (mathematically), but when he sees it, he cannot recognize it. When statisticians try their hand at spot-the-odd-item exercises as you just did, they too concede defeat. Their solution is to pretest new items in an experimental section before including them in real exams; they forgo subjective judgment, allowing actual test scores to reveal unfair items. So even though performance in the experimental SAT section does not affect anyone's test score directly, it has a profound effect on what items will appear in future versions of the test. Because test takers do not know which section is experimental, test developers can assume they exert the same effort on the experimental section as on other sections.

~ *tt tt tt* ~

Constructing SAT test forms, assembling the test items, is a massive undertaking well concealed from the casual test taker. Dozens of statisticians at ETS fuss over minute details of a test form, because decades of experience have taught them that the design of the test itself may undesirably affect scores. They know that changing the order of questions can alter scores, all else being equal, and so can replacing a single word in an item, shuffling the answer choices, or using specialist language. Therefore, much care goes into selecting and arranging test items. In any year, hundreds of new questions enter the item bank. It takes at least eighteen months for a new item to find its way onto a real test. Each item must pass six to eight reviews, with about 30 percent failing to survive.

There are people whose full-time job is to write new SAT questions. The typical item writer is middle-aged, a former teacher or school administrator, and from the middle class. If anything, the writers are extremely dedicated to their work. Chancey Jones, the retired executive director of test development at ETS, fondly recalled one of his earliest experiences with the company: "[My mentor] told me to keep a pad right by the shower. Sure enough, I came up with items when taking a shower, and I wrote them down right away. I still keep Post-Its everywhere. You never know."

One of Jones's key responsibilities was to ensure that all SAT questions were fair; in particular, no one should be disadvantaged merely by the way a test item was written or presented. Before the 1980s, the statisticians steadfastly abided by a "don't ask, don't tell" brand of ethic. Test developers believed that, because they wore race blinders, their handiwork was unaffected by the racial dimension and, ipso facto, was fair to all racial groups. Transmitting a total trust in their own creation, they viewed the SAT score as a pure measure of ability, so a differential between two scores was interpreted as a difference in ability between two examinees and nothing more. It did not occur to them to ask whether a score differential could result from unfair test items. The statisticians presumed they did no harm; they certainly meant no harm.

Our set of sample questions had already passed several preliminary filters for validity before it got screened for fairness. The items were neither too easy nor too difficult; if everyone—or no one—knew the right answer, that question had nothing to say about the difference in ability between students. Also pruned were motley items offensive to ETS, such as elitist words (*regatta, polo*), legal terms (*subpoena, tort*), religion-specific words, regionalisms (*hoagie, submarine*), and words about farms, machinery, and vehicles (*thresher, torque, strut*), plus any mention of abortion, contraception, hunting, witchcraft, and the like, all deemed "controversial, inflammatory, offensive or upsetting" to students.

~ # # # ~

Rooney did to standardized testing what he would later do to hospital bills. He rounded up an elephant of a problem and dropped it in the center of the room. The gap between blacks and whites in test scores had been evident for as long as score statistics have been published. It was not something new that emerged after Rooney filed his lawsuit. Harvard professor Daniel Koretz, in his book *Measuring Up*, acknowledges, "The difference has been large in every credible study of representative groups of school-age students." Koretz further estimated that, in the best case, the score of the *average* black student fell below 75 percent of whites. According to ETS, the average SAT scores for blacks and whites, respectively, in 2006 were 434 and 527 in reading, and 429 and 536 in mathematics.

How the racial gap in scores should be interpreted is an extremely challenging and contentious matter for all concerned. Conceptually, group differences in test scores may arise from unequal ability, unfair test construction, or some combination of both. Prior to the Golden Rule settlement, the psychometrics profession was convinced that its "don't ask, don't tell" policy produced fair tests, so score differentials could largely equate to unequal ability. Educators generally agreed that African-Americans had inferior access to high-caliber educational resources, such as well-funded schools, top ranked teachers, small classes, effective curricula, and state-of-the-art facilities, a condition that guaranteed a handicap in ability, which in turn begat the racial gap in test scores. Rooney and his supporters rejected this line of logic, arguing that score differentials were artifacts of unfair tests, which systematically underestimated the true ability of black examinees. In all likelihood, both extreme views had it wrong, and both factors contributed in part to the racial gap. This debate would not be settled until someone figured out how to untangle the two competing factors.

~ # # # ~

At the time Patrick Rooney sued ETS in 1976, the vetting of test questions for fairness was practiced as a craft, informally and without standards or documentation. The Golden Rule settlement became the first attempt to formalize the fairness review process. Further, it mandated explicit consideration of race in the development of tests. In a break from the past, ETS agreed to collect demographic data on test takers and to issue regular reports on the comparative scores of different groups. There followed a period of spectacular advance in scientific techniques to measure fairness. By 1989, test developers at ETS had broadly adopted the technical approach known as differential item functioning (DIF) analysis to augment the traditional judgmental process.

Brokered in 1984 between Rooney and Greg Anrig, the former president of ETS, the Golden Rule settlement imposed two chief conditions for validity on every test item: the overall correct rate must exceed 40 percent, and the correct rate for blacks must fall within 15 percent of that for whites. Thus, if 60 percent of whites answered a question correctly, then at least 45 percent of blacks must also have scored in order to qualify this particular item. These new rules were originally developed for the Illinois insurance licensing exam, but several states began to explore applications in educational and other testing.

Within three years, however, Anrig was to concede publicly that the Golden Rule settlement had been a "mistake." Why did this about-face occur?

Researchers reported that the new scientific review would have cast doubt on 70 percent of the verbal items on past SAT tests they reexamined. While inspecting many of the offending items that appeared to favor whites, test developers were baffled to identify what *about* them could have disadvantaged blacks. In practice, the Golden Rule procedure produced many false alarms: statisticians feared that hosts of perfectly fair questions would be arbitrarily rejected. The settlement significantly expanded the ability to identify potentially unfair test items, but it offered no help in explaining why they were unfair.

Consider sample item 3. Suppose substantially fewer boys than girls got the right answer (denoted by the asterisk). What might account for this difference in correct rates?

3. MONEY:WALLET
   A. rifle:trigger
   B. dart:spear
   C. arrow:quiver (★)
   D. golf:course
   E. football:goalpost

Perhaps boys, being generally more active, gravitated to choices that mentioned popular sports like golf and football. Perhaps more girls fell for Robin Hood–style folklore, where they encountered a word like *quiver*. Ten people would likely come up with ten narratives.

Lloyd Bond, the education scholar, frowned upon this type of judgmental review. He once relayed an enlightening story in which he and his graduate student developed elaborate reasons why certain test items favored one group of examinees, only to later discover that they had accidentally flipped the direction of the preference, and were further embarrassed when they had to reverse the previous points to support the now-reversed position. What if item 3 actually favored boys rather than girls? What might account for this difference in correct rates? Perhaps boys, being more active, grasped the relationship between *golf* and *course* and between *football* and *goalpost*, so they were *less* affected by those distracters. Perhaps fewer girls were familiar with military words like *quiver* and *rifle*. The trouble is that our fertile imagination frequently leads us astray. (By the way, girls underperformed boys by 20 percent on item 3 in real tests.)

If reasonable people could not ascertain the source of unfairness even after a test item showed a difference between groups, there was no reasonable basis on which to accuse test developers of malpractice. The problem of false alarms demonstrated that some group differences were not caused by test developers but by differential ability, elevating the need to untangle the two factors.

Henceforth, the mere existence of a racial gap should not automatically implicate item writers in the creation of unfair tests. While the initial foray into the scientific method turned out bad science, it nevertheless produced some good data, paving the way to rampant technical progress. By 1987, Anrig could turn his back on the Golden Rule procedure because the team at ETS had achieved the breakthrough needed to unravel the two factors.

Simply put, the key insight was to compare like with like. The statisticians learned not to carelessly lump together examinees with varying levels of ability. Before computing correct rates, they now match students with similar ability. High-ability whites should be compared with high-ability blacks, and low-ability whites with low-ability blacks. A test item is said to favor whites only if black examinees tend to have greater difficulty with it than whites of comparable ability. The blame can be safely assigned to test developers when two groups with like ability perform differently on the same test item, since the matching process has made moot any gap in ability. In this way, a light touch of statistical analysis unbundled the two intertwined factors.

In hindsight, statisticians added just three extra words ("of comparable ability") to the Golden Rule settlement and made a world of difference. Anrig realized belatedly that the flawed Golden Rule procedure incorporated the hidden and untenable assumption that white and black examinees were identical, and thus comparable, except for the color of their skin. In reality, the two groups should not be compared directly, because blacks were overrepresented among lower-ability students, and whites overrepresented among higher-ability students. As a result, the correct rate of white examinees leaned toward that of high-ability students, while the correct rate of black examinees leaned toward that of low-ability students. The differential mix of ability levels effected a group difference in correct rates—it would not have mattered if high-ability blacks performed just as well as high-ability whites, and likewise, low-ability blacks and low-ability whites.

It was this important breakthrough, known as DIF analysis, that finally made the scientific review of test fairness practical. Today, statisticians use it to flag a reasonable number of suspicious items for further review. A question that "shows DIF" is one in which a certain group of examinees—say, boys—performs worse than another group of like ability. Of course, explicating the source of unfairness remains as slippery as ever. In addressing this task, two test developers at ETS, Edward Curley and Alicia Schmitt, took advantage of the "experimental" SAT sections to test variations of verbal questions previously shown to be unfair. How good were their theories for why certain groups performed worse than others? Could they neutralize a bad item by removing the source of unfairness?

Our list of sample test items provided a few clues. They were, in fact, extracted from Curley and Schmitt's research. Results from real SAT tests indicated that items 1, 3, and 5 showed DIF, while the three even-numbered items did not. (Did these match your intuition?)

First, consider the DYE:FABRIC analogy (item 4). Eighty percent of all students answered this question correctly, every racial group performed just as well as whites, and girls did just as well as boys.

4. DYE:FABRIC
   A. thinner:stain
   B. oil:skin
   C. paint:wood (★)
   D. fuel:engine
   E. ink:pen

A variant of this item (4-b), with the words *paint* and *stain* interchanged, also presented minimal difficulty, with an overall correct rate of 86 percent.

4-b. DYE:FABRIC
A. thinner:paint
B. oil:skin
C. stain:wood (★)
D. fuel:engine
E. ink:pen

However, this variant was found to favor whites over every other racial group with comparable ability by 11 to 15 percent, an alarming differential. This result confirmed the hypothesis that the secondary meaning of the word *stain* could flummox nonwhite test takers. If the goal of the question was to assess recognition of word relationships rather than knowledge of vocabulary, then item 4 would be vastly preferred to item 4-b.

Next, look at item 5, which all examinees found to be very hard (17 percent correct):

5. In the past the general had been _____ for his emphasis on defensive strategies, but he was _____ when doctrines emphasizing aggression were discredited.
A. criticized . . . discharged
B. parodied . . . ostracized
C. supported . . . disappointed
D. spurned . . . vindicated (★)
E. praised . . . disregarded

Remarkably, all racial groups performed as well as whites of comparable ability, but girls appeared disadvantaged against boys of like ability by 11 percent. Researchers believed that unfairness arose from the association with conflict and tried switching the context to economics (item 5-b):

5-b. Heretofore _____ for her emphasis on
conservation, the economist was _____
when doctrines emphasizing consumption were
discredited.
A. criticized . . . discharged
B. parodied . . . ostracized
C. supported . . . disappointed
D. spurned . . . vindicated (★)
E. praised . . . disregarded

With this change, the group difference shrank to 5 percent. Recall that this 5 percent was calculated after matching ability: in practice, this meant Curley and Schmitt rebalanced the mix of ability levels of boys to mimic those of girls.

Item 1 showed an unusual racial DIF: the proportion of blacks answering correctly exceeded that of like-ability whites by an eye-popping 21 percent.

1. PLAIT:HAIR
A. knead:bread
B. weave:yarn (★)
C. cut:cloth
D. fold:paper
E. frame:picture

In hindsight, it appeared that the word *plait* might be more common in the African-American community. Researchers tried using *braid* instead (item 1-b):

1-b. BRAID:HAIR
    A. knead:bread
    B. weave:yarn (★)
    C. cut:cloth
    D. fold:paper
    E. frame:picture

The group difference disappeared, and not surprising, the overall difficulty plunged from 47 percent to 80 percent correct. The item writers took pains to point out that the question passed judgmental reviews before DIF analysis, once again showing how hard it was to identify questions that might favor certain groups without real test data. That the advantage, in this case, accrued to the minority group raised yet another practical challenge: should this type of item be removed from the test? Because test developers at ETS regard DIF in either direction as "invalid," their standard procedure calls for its removal.

Through iterations of testing and learning, Curley and Schmitt validated some but not all of the theories used to explain why items showed DIF; they also demonstrated that, indeed, items could be edited in a manner that disadvantaged one group against another.

While the United States is home to world-class test developers, American parents have only recently begun to express world-class angst over test scores. What might the future bring? We can do no worse than observing the Asians. In Hong Kong, some test prep tutors have achieved pop star status, their headshots plastered on gigantic billboards in the city center. Lecturers quit their university jobs, opting to "teach to the test" for better pay and, dare one say, greater respect. In Tokyo, *kyōiku* mamas (education-obsessed mothers) prepare care packages for their kids to carry to the university entrance examinations. Every January, Nestlé makes a killing because Kit Kat, its chocolate wafer bar, sounds like *kitto katsu*, which means "sure win" in Japanese. It might not be long until Dr. Octopus, the comic character, emerges as a brand of study aid, since it sounds like *okuto pasu*, or "if you put this on your desk, you will pass."

~ # # # ~

To figure out whether an SAT question favors whites over blacks, it would seem natural to compare the correct rate of whites with that of blacks. If the gap in performance is too wide, one would flag the item as unfair. In the Golden Rule settlement, instigated by Rooney, the acceptable gap was capped at 15 percent.

Remarkably, the statisticians at ETS disowned such an approach to the problem. In fact, they saw the Golden Rule procedure as a false start, merely a discredited precursor to a new science for screening out unfair test items. When it comes to group differences, statisticians always start with the question of whether or not to aggregate groups. The ETS staff noticed that the Golden Rule mandate required lumping together examinees into racial groups regardless of ability, which stamped out the diversity of ability levels among test takers, a key factor that could give rise to score differentials. They achieved a breakthrough by treating high-ability students and low-ability students as distinct groups. The procedure of matching ability between black and white examinees served to create groups with like ability, so any difference in correct rates signaled unfairness in the design of the test question. This so-called DIF analysis addressed the unwelcome reality that black students were already disadvantaged by inferior educational opportunities, which meant they were already suffering lower test scores, even without injustice traced to test construction.

In the course of creating the new techniques, test developers realized how hopeless it was to use their intuition to pick out unfair questions, and they smartly let actual test results guide their decisions. By placing new items in experimental test sections, they observe directly how students perform in real-life situations, eliminating any guessing. Pinpointing the source of unfair treatment is sometimes still elusive, but items that show positive or negative

DIF are typically dropped whether or not an explanation can be proffered.

The issue of group differences is fundamental to statistical thinking. The heart of this matter concerns which groups should be aggregated and which shouldn't. In analyzing standardized test scores, the statisticians strayed from what might be regarded as the natural course of comparing racial groups in aggregate. They stressed that all black examinees should not be considered as one—and neither should white examinees—because of the wide range in ability levels. (However, if the mix of ability was similar across races, the statisticians would have chosen to lump them together.)

In general, the dilemma of being together or not awaits those investigating group differences. We will next encounter it in Florida, where the hurricane insurance industry finally woke up to this problem after repeatedly losing tens of billions in single years.

~ # # # ~

Like J. Patrick Rooney, Bill Poe Sr. was also an accomplished entrepreneur who built and ran an insurance business that was eventually worth many millions of dollars. Like Rooney, he also spent his personal wealth pursuing public causes.

Poe enlivened the airwaves in 1996 when he poured $1 million of his own money into opposing public funding of a new stadium for the Tampa Bay Buccaneers football team. He filed a lawsuit against all involved parties that went up to the Florida Supreme Court, where he lost the decision. A native of Tampa, Poe was heavily involved in local politics, including a stint as mayor. In his professional life, he made a career of selling and underwriting property insurance. His first business venture was a runaway success, rapidly becoming the largest insurance brokerage in Florida. When he retired, he sold his ownership stake for around $40 million. By 2005, he made the news yet again, but in a less illustrious manner. His newest insurance venture, Poe Financial, buckled after a string of eight hurricanes battered the Florida coast in the course of two years. While Poe's customers vilified him, many of his peers sympathized, convinced that it was the breakdown of the disaster insurance market that had precipitated Poe's downfall. Indeed, as Poe had prospered in the prior decade, other insurers, particularly the national giants such as State Farm, were plotting their exits from the Sunshine State.

These developments made it increasingly certain that the average Florida resident would, willingly or not, subsidize those who choose to live near the vulnerable coast. We will now examine why.

~ # # # ~

In his native Tampa, Bill Poe was well known as a former mayor and a gifted insurance man. He founded Poe & Associates in 1956, and under his leadership, it became the largest insurance brokerage in Florida. In 1993, he negotiated a merger with Brown & Brown, the next largest competitor. Three years later, Poe retired, selling his shares for $40 million. But not for long did he stand on the sidelines. Partnering with his son, Bill Jr., he next created Southern Family Insurance Company, jumping from selling to underwriting insurance. As underwriters, the Poes took on the tasks of evaluating risks, setting premium amounts, and reserving surplus in order to cover claims.

At the time, national insurance giants like State Farm and Allstate were ruminating openly about quitting the Florida market after taking knee-bending losses from Hurricane Andrew in 1992. Having inherited hundreds of thousands of policies from failed property insurers, the state government realized it lacked sufficient capital to cover potential losses and was offering to pay start-up companies to "take out" and assume these policies. Poe was one of the early takers; on day one, Southern Family burst out with seventy thousand customers, who forked over $32 million of annual premiums to insure $6 billion worth of property, primarily in coastal areas, where the chance of a hurricane landing was the highest. For his trouble, the Florida state paid Poe over $7 million, or about $100 per policy transferred. In a startling move, Poe slashed rates by 30 percent for these customers, even as other take-out companies generally hiked prices, believing that the government had artificially capped rates before, due to political pressure. By positioning itself as a price leader and expanding through acquisitions, Poe Financial Group, operating under Southern Family and two other brands, emerged as Florida's biggest privately held property insurer by 2004, when it serviced 330,000 policies, collected premiums on the order of $300 million per year, and took on $70 billion of exposure. These results represented a phenomenal growth of 40 percent per year for eight straight years. What's more, the business produced over $100 million of profits since inception.

Then an ill wind named Wilma cleared the deck. Hurricane Wilma arrived at the tail end of two consecutive devastating seasons in which eight hurricanes battered the Florida coast. Poe Financial barely survived 2004: after paying out $800 million in claims, the company showed less than $50 million of capital on its balance sheet. In 2005, it frantically searched for fresh funds while also winning new customers to amass premiums. Neither Bill Poe nor others predicted that one horror would segue to another so that in twenty-four months, his customers suffered losses topping $2.6 billion. It was just a matter of time before Poe became insolvent. In 2005, the upstart lost more money than it had ever made in its ten-year history.

~ # # # ~

Pondering his misfortune, Bill Poe said, "This was the most unusual wind pattern in the world. The underwriter on that issue is God." Before 2004, few would have bet against Poe. With over forty years of experience, he knew the Florida market as well as anyone. Having served as Tampa's mayor, he had reliable connections and understood the regulatory environment. Almost all his customers were sourced from the state under its generous take-out policy. He then transferred most of his exposure to foreigners via reinsurance contracts. (Reinsurers insure the insurers.) As required by law, he used quantitative models to demonstrate that the firm held sufficient surplus to cope with a 100-year storm. Poe evidently followed the rules, yet the company crashed. What went wrong?

By any measure, the 2004 and 2005 seasons were extraordinary. Charley, Frances, Ivan, Jeanne, Dennis, Katrina, Rita, and Wilma: these were ill winds that showed no mercy. The Atlantic basin endured the most storms, the most hurricanes, and the most destructive hurricanes, including the single most expensive (Katrina) and the strongest (Wilma) since records began in 1850. The losses suffered in 2004–2005 erased all the profits earned by insurers in Florida since 1993. In response, the national insurance giants began to rewrite the terms of business with their customers. Property owners with existing contracts were socked with harsh price increases of as much as 200 percent, dramatic reductions in coverage, sharp hikes in deductibles, or all of these. For example, Allstate bumped rates by 8.6 percent in 2005 and 24 percent in 2006. In addition to cherry-picking the lower-risk customers, the insurers terminated outright at least half a million policies, while no other private insurer stepped forward to fill the void. When Florida prevented State Farm from charging an extra 47 percent in late 2008, the company announced its intention to abandon every one of its 700,000 customers. A sure symptom of dysfunction was when the market said no at any price. Industry leaders were acting as if hurricane risk in Florida was uninsurable.

In an editorial titled "A Failed Insurance Market," the *St. Petersburg Times* concluded, "Hope and prayer for another hurricane-free season are the only things standing between Florida and financial disaster." The market was in a crisis—an existential crisis, to be exact. At this very moment, having witnessed the ravages of deadly storms, eager customers of hurricane insurance were easy to come by. Curiously, private enterprises no longer desired to play a role, and they called on the government to pick up the slack. The problem went far beyond the collapse of Poe Financial. If hurricane risk was insurable before, why did it suddenly become uninsurable?

~ # # # ~

To get a satisfactory answer, we must first ask why anyone buys insurance and what keeps someone buying. Insurance is a thoroughly human response to the challenge of hazards: random events like hailstorms and rockfalls deplete wealth arbitrarily. People who believe in insurance contribute to a pool of funds in advance, to be drawn upon by the unfortunate afflicted. Insurance sidesteps the hopeless problem of predicting victims; instead, we let the lucky majority subsidize the unlucky few. This form of subsidy works because no member of a risk pool is immune to misfortune, and anyone can be either a donor or a beneficiary. In this sense, the arrangement is fair. By contrast, a progressive tax system or a bail-out of Wall Street stipulates a subsidy scheme under which winners and losers are predetermined. Who would voluntarily participate in such an arrangement, knowing one is almost sure to lose?

Automotive insurance is an example of a well-functioning market. In shifting their risks to insurers, drivers agree to pay premiums, most of which accumulate in a surplus account. Professionally qualified actuaries set the rates of payment at levels that should cover potential claims on average, as well as in any year. Beating the average is not good enough (witness Bill Poe); if and when payouts empty the cash vault, it is game over. Thus, a lot of care goes into designing risk pools. All members should face similar degrees of risk, or else some will tap the surplus more extensively than others. Small gaps in risk exposure are bridged by having less-safe drivers pay higher rates. Large gaps chase away safe drivers, who may feel they are paying more than their fair share, and also attract more risky drivers hoping to receive more than they put in. Since actual automotive claims have held steady over time, the actuaries are reasonably confident in their projections of future losses. In particular, they know that only a small portion of their policyholders will file claims in any given year; if everyone needed a payout immediately, the insurers would surely go bust.

Shell-shocked by the staggering losses in Florida, the hurricane insurers argued that they must have mispriced their product for years. The modeling firms that supplied them with estimates of expected losses were quick to second this view. Ernst Rauch from Munich Re, one of the two largest reinsurers in the world, reported, "Commercial modeling software of the 2005 generation put the annual loss expectancy for the USA Hurricane risk at $6 to $8 billion," which, in hindsight, ought to be described as catastrophically wrong. Based on this assumption, the insurance community requested annual payments of $10 billion from policyholders in Florida, only to suffer an actual loss of $36 billion in a mere two seasons. Warren Buffett, who knows a thing or two about the insurance business, cautioned against unfounded optimism: "Too often, insurers behave like the fellow in a switchblade fight who, after his opponent has taken a mighty swipe at his throat, exclaimed, 'You never touched me.' His adversary's reply: 'Just wait until you try to shake your head.'"

Writer Michael Lewis, in a feature article in New York Times Magazine, vividly charted how quantitative storm models rose to prominence in the mid-1990s after they had correctly predicted the unprecedented losses due to Hurricane Andrew. Their track record since then has been rather unglamorous. After admitting that it significantly underestimated the impact of the 2004–2005 hurricanes, Risk Management Solutions, the leading modeling firm, made fundamental changes to its methodology, incorporating the judgment of a panel of experts. Many of these scientists opined that climate change has rendered Atlantic hurricanes more ferocious and more frequent. With each refinement, the modelers lifted their estimates of future losses, which justified higher and higher premiums. By the late 2000s, the insurance industry asserted that to have a chance of covering projected losses, companies would have to set annual payments above what customers could reasonably afford.

Another reason why the industry grossly misjudged the level of risk was its fixation with the "100-year" storm, commonly defined as a storm of such power that it will appear only once every 100 years. In Florida, all underwriters must prove that their capital structure can withstand a 100-year storm. This rule appeared watertight as even Hurricane Andrew, which cost insurers $17 billion in 1992, was a 60-year storm. (A 100-year storm, while producing more damage than a 60-year storm, is less likely to occur.) It was unimaginable for two once-in-a-century disasters to happen in adjacent years.

Statisticians tell us that the concept of a 100-year storm concerns probability, not frequency; the yardstick is economic losses, not calendar years. They say the 100-year hurricane is one that wreaks more economic destruction than 99 percent of hurricanes in history. In any given year, the chance is 1 percent that a hurricane making landfall will produce greater losses than 99 percent of past hurricanes. This last statement is often equated to "once in a century." But consider this: if, for each year, the probability of a 100-year hurricane is 1 percent, then over ten years, the chance of seeing one or more 100-year hurricanes must cumulate to more than 1 percent (a simplified calculation puts the risk at about 10 percent). Thus, we should be less than surprised when powerful hurricanes strike Florida in succession. The "100-year" hurricane is a misnomer, granting us a false sense of security.

From the industry's perspective, the 2004–2005 disasters exposed the inadequacy of the prevailing insurance rates, which relied on wayward projections of the frequency of storms and the intensity of losses. The insurers also discovered that their customers could not bear the full cost of the insurance, so they could see no profit motive, and thus the insurance market failed.

~ # # # ~

Statisticians have something else to add to this story: Natural-disaster insurers, unlike automotive insurers, have no choice but to accept risks that are concentrated in vulnerable geographies. This agglomeration of risk became more and more severe as the existing risk pools disintegrated after the 2004–2005 seasons.

That Poe Financial shuttered in Wilma's wake had much to do with its ill-advised concentration of risks in South Florida. The two infamous seasons yielded 120,000 claims. This is to say, almost two out of five Poe customers dipped into the surplus *at the same time.* Such a massive coincidental draw on liquidity would have sunk any insurer. For this, Poe had only its flawed vision to blame. The take-out deals with the state government bloated its accounts with customers from previously failed insurers, chiefly coastal properties with the greatest chance of damage. Worse still, by competing on price, Poe violated Warren Buffett's first principle of underwriting. He once advised that if "winning" is equated with market share rather than profits, trouble awaits; "no" must be an important part of any underwriter's vocabulary. Even the last-ditch expansion effort after the 2004 hurricanes hastened Poe's demise: with new customers came more revenues but also more exposure and further accumulation of risk, compounding the original problem.

Because natural disasters strike locally, these risk pools are much less spatially diversified than those assembled by automotive insurers. Nonetheless, the principle of insurance still applies: these pools must contain some customers who would not require payment during hurricane seasons, or else simultaneous claims would bury the insurers. Traditionally, such customers included policyholders in inland Florida, other states, and foreign countries. To hear it from Bob Hartwig, the industry economist, because all Floridians belonged to the same risk pool, trailer-park grandmas were subsidizing wealthy owners of estates by the sea. Meanwhile, large national insurers borrowed surplus from other lines of business and income from other states to pay claims in Florida. When primary insurers transferred risk to reinsurers, they in effect bought the right to utilize pools of funds contributed by policyholders in other countries such as those insuring against windstorms in Europe or earthquakes in Japan. This means whenever a hurricane strikes Florida, the Europeans and Japanese effectively subsidize U.S. reconstruction projects.

Signs after 2005 indicated that none of the three groups would stick around, and for good reason. The skewed statistics of past mega-catastrophes revealed the inconvenient truth about the winners and losers of the existing insurance arrangements. Of the ten most costly disasters between 1970 and 2005, the top eight occurred in the United States, producing over 90 percent of the $176 million total insured losses; the other two included a typhoon in Japan and a windstorm in Europe. Six of those eight American disasters were Atlantic hurricanes, all of which passed through Florida. Towers Perrin, the global management and actuarial consultancy, estimated that the United States accounted for half of the premiums but three-quarters of the losses in the London reinsurance market. If this level of imbalance persists, other participants will perceive the arrangement to be unfair.

Already the market has adjusted to the new reality in various ways. The national insurance giants created Florida-only subsidiaries known as "pup companies" to protect their corporate parents, signaling their reluctance to share surplus across state lines. Reinsurers doubled rates they charge hurricane insurers based on the view that hurricane intensity and frequency have grown irreversibly. Unless the recent trend of foreigners subsidizing American disaster claims is reversed, it is hard to see how foreigners will stay in the reinsurance schemes without demanding eye-popping rate hikes, if at all.

Florida's inland residents are also likely to bail out of the risk pool, now that its inherent inequity has been laid bare. In the case of Poe Financial, 40 percent of the customer base cleaned up ten years' worth of surplus within two seasons. When coastal and inland properties are treated similarly, every policyholder pitches in the same premium, based on the *average* exposure to risk. In reality, inland properties have a much lower exposure than coastal buildings, so the low-risk residents are subsidizing the high-risk coast dwellers. As participants have widely varying exposure, the winners and losers in this risk pool are predetermined, and not surprisingly, the low-risk group of customers rejects this subsidy structure as inequitable and illegitimate. Undifferentiated risk pools could not hold together because of large group differences; as unhappy customers decamped, the remaining risk became more and more concentrated.

~ # # # ~

Just as the Golden Rule lawsuit prompted developers of standardized tests to start treating high-ability and low-ability students as distinct groups, in the aftermath of the jaw-dropping losses from 2004 2005, the insurance industry reacted by splitting the risk pool into two, a strategy statisticians refer to as stratification. After all, one can forcibly mix oil and water temporarily, but they eventually separate into layers. The insurers now fight for low-risk customers while ceding the high-risk coastal properties. How are the two groups faring under this new arrangement?

Recall that Poe Financial Group was the poster child for the take-out program initiated by the Florida government after 1992 to divest high-risk policies. The government's buildup of 1.5 million accounts was reduced to 815,000 by February 2005. Almost all of Bill Poe's customers came from this incentive program. With Poe's insolvency, it was a case of return to sender: in one swoop,

Citizens Property Insurance Corporation, the state-run caretaker, added 330,000 customers to its roster. Citizens was ill placed to handle this influx: it was about half a billion dollars in the red after the 2004 hurricane season, and the fiscal deficit ballooned to $1.7 billion by the end of 2005, even before absorbing Poe.

Having announced its conviction to bail out the Poe customers, the government was forced to raise the payout amount year after year as closed cases were reopened and new claims materialized. By late 2008, Citizens was collecting $4 billion of annual premiums but covered exposure worth $440 billion. The entity would have folded if it were a private concern. Instead, Florida legislators plugged the hole by levying a series of "assessment fees." After appropriating $920 million from the 2006 state budget, they still had to charge every buyer of homeowner or automotive insurance in the state a fee equal to 6.8 percent of premiums. For those with property insurance, this came on top of a 2 percent levy. Further, a charge of 2.5 percent would then kick in for ten years. In 2007, another 1.4 percent had to be assessed. In addition, having raised nearly $2 billion by selling bonds in 2006 and 2008, the state covered interest payments by taking another 1 percent of premiums for the next eight years. A reporter reminded her fellow Floridians in 2008, "That sucking sound you hear is a 3-year-old hurricane pulling money out of your wallet."

In a time-honored game of passing the buck, the unwanted risks were shoved from owners of seaside properties to private insurers to state-run Citizens to Bill Poe back to Citizens and finally to Floridians. For those living on the coast, nothing has changed: every year, they wish for a quiet hurricane season. When the insurers raise rates, they put up with it; when one insurer takes off, they scramble to another. As for the inland residents, they subsidized the coastal customers when private insurers used to place both groups in the same risk pool; now the state government takes their money via assessments and sends it to the coast. Same difference.

~ *# # #* ~

In an ominous development, the state government rightly got scared of the possible insolvency of Citizens should another mega-hurricane strike Florida but then promptly repeated its mistake of enticing start-up companies to take out policies from the caretaker agency. From 2006 to 2008, 800,000 policies were taken out and taken up by bit players who received "D" (weak) or "E" (very weak) grades from rating agencies, due to inadequate capital and inexperience. The state regulator took a farcical position: "Could there be another monster like Katrina or worse? God forbid if there were. All bets would be off at that point." We've seen this script before, and it did not have a happy ending.

And the troubles do not end there. One might expect the devastation wrought by Hurricane Wilma to have deterred Floridians from moving to the coast, but the trend has showed no sign of easing. Economists blame "moral hazard": coastal dwellers are less worried about hurricanes because they expect the state to continue the unending bailouts and offer an implicit backstop. New residents believe that if their homes should fall, someone else will pay for the reconstruction, so why not enjoy living along the coast? This alarming trend further aggravates the economics of hurricane insurance. The already heavy concentration of simultaneous risks has gained even more heft. The increased population density inflates real estate prices so that the number of risks multiplied by the value of each exposure has expanded by leaps and bounds. Many scientists consider the "lemming-like march to the sea" as a much more serious threat than the recent rise in intensity and frequency of hurricanes. By 2006, Florida owned $2.5 trillion of insured properties, the largest value of any state, eclipsing even New York. Storm models predicted that a hurricane of Katrina's strength would produce upwards of $100 billion in losses if it traversed the Miami area, repeating the disaster of 1926. While this threat looms, the insurance market in Florida stands paralyzed.

~###~

The harrowing hurricane seasons of 2004–2005 awakened the disaster insurance industry to an essential reality: under existing risk pools, customers with low-risk inland properties were sure losers, and those with high-risk coastal properties sure winners. This group difference threatened the viability of the insurance arrangements because the cross-subsidies no longer appeared fair. The big insurers reacted by imposing stunning rate hikes, especially on the high-risk group, in effect shutting them out. When the state regulator objected, they relinquished the entire market. Inevitably, the state of Florida assumed the role of insurer of last resort, which did nothing to relieve the low-risk group from subsidizing the coastal property owners. If the state must play such a role, then it must provide incentives to slow the migration of people and wealth to the vulnerable coastline. If the state cannot or will not stop the unfair cross-subsidies, it must at least respect the low-risk residents by working to ease their burden. When past lessons are not learned, the next disaster is only a matter of time.

On the surface, the insurer and the test developer have nothing in common: one assembles a profitable roster of customers, while the other constructs a fair set of test questions. From a statistical point of view, they both have to grapple with the issue of group differences. In both cases, variability across groups was seen as undesirable. Test developers made a breakthrough when they understood that they could not directly compare black students with white students; by contrast, an insurance market verged on disintegrating once insurers realized that they could not treat every customer as the average customer. The crucial decision in these situations is whether or not one should aggregate groups. That is the dilemma of being lumped together.

4

Timid Testers / Magic Lassos

The Sway of Being Asymmetric

I want to talk about the positive, not the negative, about this issue.
—MARK McGWIRE, PROFESSIONAL BASEBALL PLAYER

You don't even have to know what it is you're searching for. But you'll know it once you find it.
—CRAIG NORRIS, CEO OF ATTENSITY

A watershed occurred in the early 2000s, when the base-ball players' union finally acquiesced to a steroid-testing program. Baseball fans were losing faith in the integrity of the national pastime, and the scandal was fueled by a pair of sensational books: *Juiced*, in which All-Star slugger Jose Canseco exposed himself as the "Godfather of Steroids" and outed several well-loved ballplayers as dopers, and *Game of Shadows*, in which two *San Francisco Chronicle* reporters laid bare the federal investigation of BALCO, a California supplier of steroids to many elite athletes, including baseball players. It was no longer possible to deny that performance-enhancing drugs had infiltrated the sport, just as they had cycling and track.

Drug use is harmful to the athlete and makes a mockery of the sporting spirit. Most sports have adopted an anti-doping code written by the World Anti-Doping Agency (WADA), requiring athletes to submit urine or blood samples for testing. Baseball's steroid-testing program, however, does not meet the more stringent international standard, as grudging players opt to take one small step at a time. For example, Major League Baseball (MLB) does not test for human growth hormone (HGH), a powerful drug that burst on the scene in the late 1990s. Boston Red Sox star Mike Lowell explained why: "[HGH testing] has to be 100 percent accurate, because if it's 99 percent accurate, there are going to be seven false positives in big league baseball, and what if any of those names is one of the major names?"

Baseball salary statistics fanned Lowell's uneasiness: the average MLB player earned almost $2.5 million in 2005, and Lowell's team, the Red Sox, was one of the league's wealthiest, paying more than $4 million per athlete. With so much money at stake, it is no wonder that ballplayers are worried sick about false-positive errors in steroid testing—about drug-free athletes who get falsely accused. However, with the focus squarely on this one aspect of testing, the anti-doping community has unintentionally abetted the drug cheats. In this chapter, we will learn how.

A variation of the steroid detection problem disquieted American troops stationed in Iraq and Afghanistan: how to screen large numbers of local job applicants for past, present, or future association with insurgency. At Camp Cropper in Iraq, David Thompson led a team of interrogators who relied on their training, real-world experience, and gut instinct to "filter truth from fiction." This lie detection process proved imperfect as insurgents continued to target Thompson's soldiers. With each phase of the war, he noticed that the recruits arrived younger, less experienced, and thus less prepared for immediate success in the counterintelligence work.

Imagine the thrill when he received a shipment of portable lie detectors in 2007. The portable lie detector is a handheld computer with fingertip electrodes for measuring skin conductivity and pulse rate. An operator asks the subject a list of yes/no questions and taps in the answers; within minutes, the computer processes the data from the electrodes and renders a verdict: green for truthful, red for deceptive, and yellow for inconclusive. Like the conventional polygraph, this miniature version actually detects anxiety, which can be induced by either the act of lying or the fear of getting caught lying, depending on which expert we believe. Unlike users of the conventional polygraph, Thompson's interrogators no longer require expertise or real-life experience; the computer program, optimized by physicists at Johns Hopkins University, removes the human element from counterintelligence screening. Each portable lie detector costs $7,250 plus an annual maintenance fee of $600.

With many American lives at stake, it is no wonder that army leaders worry about false-negative errors in interrogations—about insurgents who evade detection during screening. They instructed the Johns Hopkins researchers to calibrate the gadget so that those who receive green lights have virtually zero chance of having lied. However, statisticians tell us that by focusing exclusively on this one aspect of accuracy, the technologists have unintentionally impaired the ability of this gadget to pick out potential suspects, its primary function. In this chapter, we will learn how.

Steroid testing and lie detection are both technologies that classify people into types: dopers versus clean athletes, liars versus truth tellers. Critics fault drug tests for destroying careers (false positives) and polygraphs for missing potential criminals (false negatives). Statisticians point out that such technologies face an undesirable but also unavoidable trade off between the two types of errors. Any detection system can be calibrated, but different settings merely redistribute errors between false positives and false negatives; it is impossible to simultaneously reduce both. As an analogy, consider a baseball hitter of average skill level: he can swing the bats more aggressively, in which case he will register more strikeouts, or less aggressively, in which case he will hit fewer home runs. More importantly, some errors are more visible and more costly than others. Such asymmetry provides strong incentives for drug testers and law enforcement officers to focus their energies on one type of error while the other aspect is neglected and unnoticed. The sway of being asymmetric is the subject of this chapter.

~ # # # ~

Mike Lowell, the professional third baseman, was considered toast in Florida before he became the toast of Boston. When the Florida Marlins traded Lowell to the Red Sox in 2005 after two consecutive under-par seasons, they felt the veteran player had seen his best years, and eagerly unloaded his $9 million annual salary to the Boston club. They could scarcely have imagined that Lowell would be named Most Valuable Player in the 2007 World Series, capping off a banner year in which he broke personal records in hits, runs batted in, batting average, and OPS (on-base plus slugging percentage) at the somewhat-old age of thirty-three. Thanks to the one scintillating season, the Red Sox rewarded Lowell with a hefty pay hike to $12 million a year. Mike Lowell's climb from the humble son of a Cuban exile and a cancer survivor to the top flight of baseball was the substance of American dreams.

For Major League Baseball, 2007 was a year in which dreams threatened to turn into mirages. While Lowell's performance on the field exhilarated Boston fans, baseball was sagging under the weight of a steroid scandal that could expose some of the game's biggest stars as frauds. The seeds were sown in 1998, when Mark McGwire and Sammy Sosa captivated crowds with a superhuman, down-to-the-wire home run chase, both of them surpassing Roger Maris's record, previously regarded as sacrosanct. The cynics whispered about rampant abuse of steroids by ballplayers inflating their statistics artificially.

Then tantalizing clues started to emerge. A bottle of andros-tenedione, a stimulant banned in the Olympics, was spotted inside McGwire's locker. When Barry Bonds shattered McGwire's record three years later, skeptics noted that the thirty-seven-year-old appeared bigger, stronger, and better than his younger self. Old-school baseball watchers wanted to embellish Bonds's record with a big black mark even before any proof came to light. Then, in 2003, federal investigators found physical evidence that a California lab, BALCO, had supplied performance-enhancing drugs to elite athletes. The used syringes, doping schedules, and client records entangled numerous ballplayers, among them super-star Bonds. Bonds later admitted to using two substances from BALCO, known as the "clear" and the "cream," but maintained he thought they were flaxseed oil and antiarthritis balm. Top track coach Trevor Graham anonymously sent a syringe of the "clear" to anti-doping authorities in a sacrificial act to knock out a rival team of athletes he knew to be fellow BALCO clients, leading to its identification as THG (tetrahydrogestrinone), a designer steroid engineered by chemists to be undetectable by testing labs.

Next, 3,000-hit man Jose Canseco blew the lid off when he alleged in his sensational 2005 book, *Juiced*, that four out of every five ballplayers, including McGwire and Jason Giambi, used ste-roids. Later that year, prompted by President George W. Bush's State of the Union address, legislators conducted congressio-nal hearings, which were most notable for McGwire's refrain, "I am not here to talk about the past. I want to talk about the positive, not the negative, about this issue." Another star slug-ger, Rafael Palmeiro, declared to Congress, "I have never used steroids, period. I don't know how to say it any more clearly than that. Never." Six months later, he tested positive for stanozolol, the same steroid found in sprinter Ben Johnson's urine at the 1988 Seoul Olympics. In 2007, young Rick Ankiel provided baseball fans with an unlikely feel-good story: the pitcher for the St. Louis

Cardinals, who in his rookie season had inexplicably lost his ability to throw strikes during the World Series, resurrected his career
by winning a starting job as a major-league hitter. The excitement
faded, however, when an investigation linked Ankiel to a Florida
clinic suspected of distributing HGH to professional athletes (the
league did not discipline him).

All of these threads were expected to converge in December
2007, when Senator George Mitchell issued his report on the steroid scandal. The nature of the evidence was as yet unknown, and
speculation was running rife that scores of players would be named
and vilified.

Such was the backdrop when Mike Lowell spoke to the Boston
chapter of the Baseball Writers Association. As befitted a college
graduate in finance, he gave a succinct, analytical rationale for why
the players, led by union chief Donald Fehr, have long vacillated
on the issue of steroid testing:

> *"[HGH testing] has to be 100 percent accurate, because if it's
> 99 percent accurate, there are going to be seven false positives in
> big league baseball, and what if any of those names is one of the
> major names? You've scarred that person's career for life. You can't
> come back and say 'Sorry, we've made a mistake,' because you just
> destroyed that person's career.*
>
> *"There's got to be 100 percent accuracy, and that's why Donald
> Fehr puts himself in a position where he's responsible for the seven
> false positives, not the 693 that test OK. Because, God forbid, what
> if it was [Hall of Fame shortstop] Cal Ripken, you know what I
> mean? Doesn't that put a big black mark on his career? That's where
> I think the union has to make sure the test is 100 percent, no chance
> of a false positive. Some people have said 90 percent [accuracy].
> That's 70 [false positives]. That's three full rosters."*

A false positive occurs when an athlete who did not cheat is falsely found to have cheated. "Being called a cheater, knowing I didn't cheat, it's the worst feeling in the world," opined Tyler Hamilton, the American cyclist who famously and valiantly endured a painful collarbone injury to finish fourth in the 2003 Tour de France. Adored by cycling fans as a straitlaced "Boy Scout" and respected by colleagues as an all-around nice guy, Hamilton was poised to emerge from the shadow of Lance Armstrong, his mentor, in 2004. His income topped $1 million, including salary and endorsement deals with Nike, Oakley, and other brands. In Athens that year, he became the first American to win an Olympic road race in twenty years.

Suddenly and cruelly, his world came crashing down as the drug testers at the Tour of Spain found foreign blood mixed with Hamilton's. The outlawed practice of transfusing another person's blood cells into one's blood, called blood doping, raises the amount of oxygen carried in one's bloodstream, a key driver of cycling ability. Subsequently, it was disclosed that the "A" sample collected from Hamilton in Athens had also raised a red flag, but the rules barred further action when the lab technician inadvertently froze the "B" sample. (To increase accuracy, testing labs divide blood or urine samples into "A" and "B" halves and declare a positive only when both parts test positive.) Defiant, Hamilton demurred, "We don't have an answer to why there was a positive test at the moment. If I knew the answer, I'd have it tattooed on my arm. The bottom line, I didn't blood dope." His lawyers advanced the possibility that the foreign blood belonged to a "vanishing twin," an abortive twin brother who might have shared a womb with Hamilton.

Hamilton's defense was as standard as it came for accused athletes: he never cheated, so the positive finding must have been a *false* positive, which could be explained by alternative causes, such as vanished twins. The arbitrator eventually rejected Hamilton's appeal, and he served a two-year ban from cycling. If he were indeed a clean athlete, his plight would justify Mike Lowell's worry about false positives ruining the supernova careers of elite athletes.

Accused athletes have had trouble shaking off the stigma of testing positive—and for good reason. Travis Tygart, CEO of the U.S. Anti-Doping Agency (USADA) once observed, "Denial is the common currency of the guilty as well as the innocent." Such behavior is consistent with their incentives. The truly innocent athlete, upon failing a drug test, should immediately hire a lawyer, find character witnesses, seek alternative explanations, challenge the lab procedures, and fight tooth and nail. The guilty athlete frequently pursues the same course of action while voluntarily withdrawing from competition. At worst, he loses the argument and gets suspended for two years, backdated to when he ceases competing, disregarding when his final appeal falls apart. If lucky, he may find exoneration via a botched procedure, a spoiled sample, or a sympathetic arbitrating judge. By a strategy of denial, the guilty athlete spends most of the suspension clearing his name with a remote chance of redemption; if he instead chooses not to contest the positive finding, humiliation arrives instantly, but reinstatement no sooner.

Consequently, the true positive and the false positive, once commingled, are difficult to set apart. That is why millionaire athletes like Mike Lowell demand nothing less than a test that is "100 percent accurate, [with] no chance of a false positive."

If only real life were so perfect.

Statisticians say even if a test committed zero false positives, it would be far from "100 percent accurate" because of false-negative errors. Athletes only complain about false positives; the media wax on about false positives. We are missing the big story of steroid testing: *false negatives.*

~ # # # ~

In an impassioned letter written in his own defense, cyclist Tyler Hamilton asserted, "I have been tested over 50 times throughout my career and this is the first time I have ever even been questioned." Actually, entire pelotons have been pedaling under a stubborn fog of suspicion ever since a string of sensational drug busts hit the sport's marquee event, the Tour de France, in the 1990s and 2000s. Second-guessing hard-to-believe performances has become a spectator sport. Protesting and proving their innocence has become a second job for many cyclists.

Hamilton's heroics at the Tour de France happened under the watch of Bjarne Riis, the owner of the CSC-sponsored team and a former champion from Denmark. Accusations also trailed Riis for a decade after his memorable and devastating victory in 1996. One observer recalled the occasion: "Through a series of a dozen or so brutally calculated accelerations and decelerations, he ripped the legs off his competition, knocking a few loose with each surge, until he ended up alone and very far ahead." This feat Riis accomplished at the age of thirty-three as the leader of a then-unheralded Telekom team, the first time he had commandeered any team in ten years of racing. As owner of the CSC team, he raised many eyebrows by assembling a front-ranked club within two years. As a rider, Riis always met his doubters with one answer: I have never tested positive. He attributed his success to bee pollen, training methods, and "Thinking to Win," and he incorporated these elements into the CSC program. In 2004, Riis denounced cheaters in a public letter: "It is—to put it mildly—extremely frustrating to experience how some within the sport do not live up to the wish that most of us have for a healthy, sound, professional sport."

Marion Jones, the superstar sprinter and *Vogue* cover girl, was certified clean in every one of about 160 samples she provided in her illustrious career. She reached dizzying heights at the 2000 Sydney Olympics, earning five medals, three of them gold. Her annual earnings, which included race bonuses and endorsement deals, exceeded $1 million. But rumors hounded her, not least because of the company she kept, particularly ex-husband C. J. Hunter, ex-boyfriend Tim Montgomery, and coach Trevor Graham. Hunter, a shot put champion, was busted when he tested positive for the steroid nandrolone at a thousand times the normal level. Montgomery, one-time 100-meter world record holder, and Graham, celebrated coach of numerous tainted athletes, were key figures in the BALCO scandal.

Notwithstanding, Jones adamantly denied ever using drugs. In her autobiography, she shouted in large, red, capital letters:

"I HAVE ALWAYS BEEN UNEQUIVOCAL IN MY OPINION: I AM AGAINST PERFORMANCE-ENHANCING DRUGS. I HAVE NEVER TAKEN THEM AND I NEVER WILL TAKE THEM."

In case we missed the message, she splattered the words all over page 173. When the owner of BALCO, Victor Conte, alleged that she doped "before, during and after the 2000 Olympics," Jones served up a $25 million defamation lawsuit. In an interview with "20/20," the public-affairs program, Conte described how Jones "did the injection with me sitting right there next to her. . . . [She] didn't like to inject in the stomach area. . . . She would do it in her quad." Her lawyers dismissed Conte as "simply not credible." When ex-husband Hunter also implicated her, she called him a vindictive liar. At a time when droves of elite track athletes were being exposed, such as double world sprint champion Kelli White, 200-meter world champion Michelle Collins, 1,500-meter world record holder Regina Jacobs, British sprinter and European record holder Dwain Chambers, and Olympic gold medalist twins Calvin and Alvin Harrison, Marion Jones stood tall, never testing positive once. She decried unjust treatment by the media, complaining, "The athletes who have not tested positive have been dragged through the mud."

Then in August 2006, Jones got a scare: an "A" sample she had provided at the U.S. championships tested positive for EPO (erythropoietin), a high-tech replica of blood doping that obviates nasty blood transfusions. Her detractors pounced while she continued to deny. Her then coach, Steve Riddick, declared, "I would stake my life on it she did not take EPO." Within a month, the "B" sample was ruled inconclusive, so for the moment, Jones's integrity remained intact.

Now her supporters had their turn to gloat. They attacked the validity of the EPO test as the positive finding of the "A" sample was overturned by the inconclusive "B" sample. Her lawyer lamented, "Marion was wrongfully accused of a doping violation and her reputation was unfairly questioned." For her part, Jones reiterated, "I have always maintained that I have never ever taken performance-enhancing drugs, and I am pleased that a scientific process has now demonstrated that fact."

What was the common link between Marion Jones and Bjarne Riis? They both scaled the summit of their sport, they both passed every drug test along the way, they both reaped the riches afforded superstars, and they both swept aside accusations with strident public declarations of honesty. Last but not least, they were disgraceful drug cheats both. Ten years after his stirring victory, long after he had quit competitive cycling, Riis publicly confessed to extensive doping, including EPO, HGH, and cortisone. Jones eventually confessed in 2007, but only after federal prosecutors had hauled her into court on perjury charges stemming from the many lies she sprang at BALCO investigators. She spent six months in jail. (By contrast, Tyler Hamilton, the clean-cut Olympic champion, never admitted to cheating; on returning to competitive cycling after the 2005 suspension, he repeatedly failed drug tests, and the eight-year ban he was served in 2009 effectively ended his career.)

Supporters of Marion Jones pointed to her ordeal at the 2006 U.S. Championships as a real example of a false-positive error. In reality, Jones tested negative at the meet owing to the inconclusive

"B" sample, which acted as an automatic protector against false positives. Given subsequent events, one must turn this around and ask if, rather than a false positive, the finding was a false negative! That scenario was more likely, even though Jones had only owned up to unintentional doping between September 2000 and July 2001 (that is, not in 2006). Like Barry Bonds, she claimed to have believed the "clear" was flaxseed oil until the BALCO scandal broke. Her many accusers, however, insisted that she had had full knowledge. Only Jones and her staff would know the whole truth.

London's *Daily Telegraph*, in assessing Jones's extravagant demise, offered this perspective: "The inconvenient truth that testing negative means nothing is really the key finding of the Marion Jones episode." The reporter was pitch perfect in her evaluation, and one wonders why few others picked up on the story. Statistical analysis shows that in steroid testing, a negative finding has far less value than a positive. As shown in Figure 4-1, for each doper caught red-handed (true positive), one should expect about ten others to have escaped scot-free (false negatives). False negatives, not false positives, are the true story of steroid testing.

In particular, pay attention to these two numbers: the proportion of samples declared positive by drug-testing laboratories and the proportion of athletes believed to be using steroids. Of thousands of tests conducted each year, typically 1 percent of samples are declared positive. Therefore, if 10 percent of athletes are drug cheats, then the vast majority—at least 9 percent of them—would have tested negative, and they would have been false negatives. (If the athletes were right that some of the positive findings were errors, then even more dopers would have been missed.)

~ # # # ~

The issue of false negatives has largely been ignored by the media and is virtually untouched by athletes. Tyler Hamilton, Marion Jones, and others contend that every negative result helped prove their innocence but no positive finding could corroborate their

Figure 4-1 How Steroid Tests Miss Ten Dopers for Each One Caught

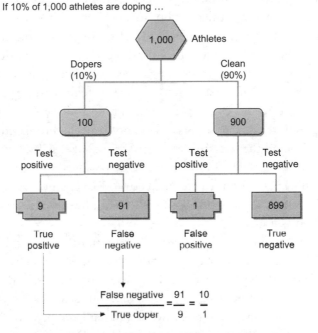

If 10% of 1,000 athletes are doping …

True positives and false positives should add up to 1% (10 positives out of 1,000 tests). Higher false positives imply lower true positives, which imply higher false negatives.

guilt. Channeling Mark McGwire, they might well have chanted, "We are here to talk about the false positive, not the false negative, about steroid testing." Mike Lowell expressed the same belief in numerical terms. Since three full rosters equaled 70 guys, and there were thirty teams in Major League Baseball, he assumed a total of 700 players, each tested once annually. Of the 700 players, 693 "tested OK," meaning they were clean; the other 7 were false positives, meaning that they too were clean. In other words, all 700 were clean, but 7 hard-luck players tested positive erroneously. With no dopers, of course, every positive result must be a false positive. In Lowell's world, the only acceptable test was the one that gave only negatives.

Some dismiss false negatives as victimless errors. Not true. As Michael Johnson, the superlative sprinter with the golden Nike spikes, wrote, "the athletes who finished behind [the winner who cheated] will never experience the glory or recoup the financial benefit they deserved for their hard work." To his credit, Johnson saw the problem of false negatives. A count of the victims of Marion Jones had to start with her relay teammates (who were required to return their medals), and then there were all the silver medalists who should have won gold, all the bronze medalists silver, and all the fourth-place finishers bronze. All waited seven years to learn they had been cheated. (In a sardonic twist, some "victims" turned out to be cheats, too. For example, four of the other seven finalists who raced with Ben Johnson have since been exposed as dopers.)

Many athletes get away with cheating. In the anti-doping community, this statement is not controversial. In a review of drug testing for the *New York Times*, Professor Charles Yesalis disclosed, "It is virtually impossible to mistakenly identify a substance if a person tests positive for it. [However,] it has been proven that testing cannot catch all substance abusers." Dr. Rasmus Damsgaard, who ran anti-doping programs for professional skiing and cycling teams, estimated that "maybe hundreds, maybe even thousands of EPO positive samples are lying around in WADA-accredited labs," that is, after having passed testing. Poring over past doping cases, perhaps David Letterman would feel inspired to make one of his famous Top Ten lists for easy tips to produce a false negative. If so, he might consult the following methods that were actually used, as presented by the athletes with firsthand experience:

10. When the tester is looking away, stir in a little whiskey, and shake it. (Irish swimmer Michelle Smith)
9. Misdirect the testers to the wrong place, and then stage a motorcycle accident to avoid the out-of-competition

test. (Sprinter Konstantinos Kederis, also known as "the greatest living Greek")

8. Hold a friend's pee inside your body, release quickly when the tester shows up. I get extra credit for being cooperative. (Russian track star Yelena Soboleva and six teammates)

7. Believe in human frailty. If a clueless lab technician freezes one of the samples, the lab cannot run a test on it. (Tyler Hamilton)

6. It's all about timing! Know how long it takes for the stuff to clear. (American sprinter Kelli White)

5. Easy does it for guys. Wear a prosthetic and give them fake pee. (Customers of the Whizzinator and similar products)

4. Be ahead of the curve; use only the newest designer stuff. They don't know what it is, so they don't test for it, wink wink. (BALCO athletes)

3. It's a natural high. The testosterone is all yours. You're just more manly than the competition. (American cyclist Floyd Landis)

2. It's so easy to walk right through the front door. Apply for the pass to cheat; it's called the therapeutic-use exemption. You have asthma, you can dope. (Many athletes)

And the number one easy tip to produce a false negative is . . . to sit back and relax, as timid testers will let cheaters ride off into the sunset for fear of wrongly besmirching honest athletes.

Could this really be true? Conventional wisdom says testers and cheaters engage in a high-tech cat-and-mouse game, in which self-righteous testers, eager—perhaps overly eager—to catch the cheaters, tend to cast a wide net, trapping many innocents. However, once we understand the incentives causing testers to look the other way, the game appears to play out differently. The testers are timid because they are swayed by asymmetric costs from the two types of error. A false positive—in fact, any positive, as Tygart observed—will be rigorously litigated by the accused. An overturned positive publicly humiliates the anti-doping authorities and diminishes the credibility of the testing program. By contrast, negative findings can only be proven false if athletes, like Riis, step forward to confess, so most false negatives never see the light of day. Athletes and testers alike can hide behind the anonymity of the false negative. The testers are timid because the false-negative error imparts negligible cost while the false positive can be highly public and highly toxic. Since anti-doping agencies pursue only the strongest cases, no wonder they have won almost all of them. Our criminal-justice system makes the same judgment call: a few murderers escape punishment so that very few innocent people are sent to the chair.

~ # # # ~

Timid testers are eager to minimize false positives. This objective doesn't conflict with the desire to avoid false-negative mistakes, or does it? Statisticians tell us it definitely does. Testers face an unsavory trade-off: fewer false positives mean more false negatives; fewer false negatives mean more false positives. We next consider how this trade-off manifests itself in steroid tests, using the hematocrit test for catching blood dopers as an illustration.

While no fewer than nine Tour de France champions have been exposed as frauds since 1975, Bjarne Riis had the distinction of carrying the nickname Mr. Sixty Percent, a sarcastic reference to his alleged hematocrit level. The hematocrit level measures the density of red blood cells as a proportion of blood volume. Normal males register a level of about 46 percent. A level of 50 percent or higher is considered abnormal, and 60 percent is insane, because blood becomes too viscous, putting enormous pressure on the heart. The effect is like sucking thick milk shake up a narrow straw.

Before more advanced tests became available, the International Cycling Union (known by its French initials, UCI) used the hematocrit test to identify suspected EPO abusers. EPO is a hormone, naturally secreted by the kidney, which stimulates the growth of red blood cells. By injecting synthetic EPO, endurance athletes boost their red cell counts (and hematocrit levels), raising the oxygen-carrying capacity of their blood. Training at altitude provides similar benefits but is inconvenient and reportedly less effective. EPO is basically the modern form of blood doping. It is also a potent killer: doctors suspect that the reason why, in recent years, a number of young cyclists—fit men in their prime—have suffered fatal heart attacks in their sleep is EPO abuse. There is a saying that "Cyclists live to ride during the day and then ride to stay alive at night." Allegedly, some EPO users wake up multiple times a night and jump on the exercise machines to get their heart rates up!

UCI used to disqualify everyone with a hematocrit level above 50 percent. This policy sidelined the dopers but also those with a "natural high"; for example, about 20 percent of people living in highlands have natural red cell densities above 50 percent, and they fell victim to the false positive. Anticipating this, UCI did not regard the positives as doping violations but instead considered the disqualification a measure to protect the health of cyclists.

Statisticians tell us it was the threshold of 50 percent used to separate natural from unnatural that fixed the unavoidable trade-off between the two types of errors. If the testers had used 60 percent, they could have reduced false positives, but without a doubt, more dopers would have evaded detection. Similarly, lowering the disqualifying hematocrit level would decrease false negatives at the expense of allowing more false positives.

Nowadays, WADA relies on a more sophisticated, more accurate urine test for EPO. Whether steroid tests measure hematocrit level or another indicator, the principle of all the tests is the same. By setting the threshold of separation, anti-doping authorities explicitly calibrate the tests according to their tolerance for each type of error. Because false positives make for lousy publicity, containing these errors is a top priority. However, this policy inevitably means some drug cheats are let loose, especially since testers can hide behind the false negatives, which are invisible. Due to the sway of asymmetric costs, testers are timid.

~ # # # ~

Even though anti-doping agencies are inclined to minimize false positives, many athletes echo Mike Lowell's fear. Rafael Palmeiro believed an injection of vitamin B_{12} caused a false positive. Tyler Hamilton said his vanished twin caused a false positive. Floyd Landis, the American cyclist, claimed a few beers caused his testosterone level to spike. Petr Korda, the Czech tennis player, believed eating veal from calves fed with nandrolone caused his positive. David Martinez, the Spanish discus thrower, citing pigs, even raised one on nandrolone to prove his point. Ben Johnson has long claimed that Carl Lewis spiked his energy drinks, causing the positive. Justin Gatlin, another American sprinter, said his masseuse rubbed steroid-laced cream on his legs. Zach Lund, the American skeleton rider, knew it was a baldness cure that put finasteride in his body. The list goes on.

We may choose to believe all, or some, of these claims. It does not matter, because from a scientific point of view, none of these results actually constituted a false positive! To see why, we must separate the test of chemistry from the test of integrity. In the test of chemistry, a false positive occurs when the testers report finding an illegal substance that, in fact, does not exist in the sample. In each of the cases just described, the athlete tacitly admitted the presence of the banned drug, so each case was a true positive, notwithstanding the colorful explanations for how steroids entered their bodies. How then do we assess the claims about nutritional supplements, spiked drinks, and so on? Can we take the athletes' words for it? This is no longer a question of the science; it falls into the realm of lie detection, which is where we now head.

~ # # # ~

The modern-day polygraph machine is a fear-inducing briefcase filled with medical diagnostic tools, including a chest cord for measuring breathing, an arm cuff for gauging blood pressure and pulse rate, and fingertip electrodes for sensing skin conductivity. Forensic psychologists believe that the act of lying or the fear of getting caught lying raises anxiety, and scientifically speaking, the polygraph detects anxiety, not actual deception. William Marston, a Harvard-trained psychologist who was the first to relate truth telling and blood pressure variations, failed to popularize the concept in the early twentieth century, but he ultimately achieved immortality by creating the comic book heroine Wonder Woman, who not coincidentally wielded a Magic Lasso that "makes all who are encircled in it tell the truth."

Rather than a "lie detector," the polygraph is simply an instrument of data collection; the data can suggest signs of anxiety, but deception is just one of various causes of elevated blood pressure, hastened breaths, and so on. Therefore, the role of the polygraph examiner is paramount in judging which apprehensive subject is a liar and which is not. A polygraph machine without a competent examiner is like a stock chart without a seasoned analyst: reams of numbers without any significance.

The typical examiner is a retired employee of a law enforcement or intelligence agency that utilizes polygraphs in conducting investigations. He or she has undertaken professional training, such as the thirteen-week course at the Polygraph Institute of the Department of Defense, followed by a six-month internship. This person has developed confidence in his or her ability to interpret fluctuations of various bodily metrics, such as pulse rate and blood pressure. To establish a baseline level of anxiety, the examiner usually engages the subject in extensive pretest conversation, including previewing the test questions. The actual test begins when the examiner feels that the subject is completely at ease. Whenever the examiner senses signs of deception, he or she suspends the test to elicit the subject's state of mind. Throughout the test, the examiner looks out for countermeasures—tactics that the subject may use to derail the examiner, such as biting one's tongue, controlling breathing, contracting certain muscles, deliberately stepping on a hidden tack inside one's shoe, counting backward, and any number of other tactics directors have popularized on film.

~ # # # ~

In 2005, the simmering steroid scandal in Major League Baseball boiled over as six-time All-Star slugger and self-appointed Godfather of Steroids Jose Canseco ignited the blowtorch known as *Juiced*, his finger-pointing exposé of the steroid subculture in baseball locker rooms. Canseco dropped bombshells such as "If I had to guess, I'd say eight out of every ten players had kits in their lockers filled with growth hormones, steroids, supplements." Of greatest interest to the media, though, he named names, starting with fan favorites, including Mark McGwire, Juan Gonzalez, Ivan Rodriguez, Rafael Palmeiro, and Jason Giambi. Regarding McGwire, Canseco recounted, "Mark and I would duck into a stall in the men's room, load up our syringes and inject ourselves. I would often inject Mark." The author of *Juiced* was promptly branded as vindictive, despicable, and delusional.

Hell hath no fury like a Godfather scorned. Three years after *Juiced*, Canesco reloaded his blowtorch, delivering a sequel called *Vindicated*. Far from repenting, he reiterated his earlier claims and even advanced some new ones, including an educated guess that Alex Rodriguez, one of the most bankable stars of baseball, was a doper.

To clear any doubts, Canseco released verbatim transcripts of two lie detector tests conducted by recognized experts. One of these, John Grogan, administered the most popular interview format, known as the Control Question Test, which mashes up three types of questions: relevant, irrelevant, and control. The following snippet came from the start of his examination of Canseco:

Grogan:	Is today Thursday? [irrelevant]
Canseco:	Yes.
Grogan:	Is your name Jose? [irrelevant]
Canseco:	Yes.
Grogan:	Did you and Mark McGwire ever have conversations about the use of steroids or human growth hormones? [relevant]
Canseco:	Yes.
Grogan:	Is your last name Canseco? [irrelevant]
Canseco:	Yes.
Grogan:	Did you ever inject Mark McGwire with steroids or human growth hormones? [relevant]
Canseco:	Yes.
Grogan:	In the last ten years, have you lied to benefit yourself financially? [control]
Canseco:	No.
Grogan:	Is your shirt black? [irrelevant]
Canseco:	Yes.

And on it went. Grogan looked for any difference in emotions when Canseco answered relevant versus control questions. "Control" questions concern vague and broad categories of wrongdoing, such as office theft and white lies, designed to make even truthful subjects experience discomfort. Liars are supposed to feel greater anxiety toward the relevant questions, while truth tellers are expected to be bothered more by control questions.

Grogan did not equivocate regarding Canseco's performance: "He's one hundred percent telling the truth on all questions regarding human growth hormones and steroids. And the computer misses nothing, not the most smallest, insignificant tracings. . . . It gave him a .01 score on every chart, which, if this was in school, would be an A-plus on every chart collected." Take that, baseball!

~ # # # ~

Many other athletes also tried to clear their names via polygraph tests. The lawyers of superstar sprinter Marion Jones, in a bid to fend off persistent rumors of her steroid use, declared that she had passed a polygraph test. Immediately, they challenged Jones's accuser-in-chief, BALCO founder Victor Conte, to submit to a polygraph himself (he never did). They taunted, "It is easy to go on national television and . . . make 'false, malicious and misleading' statements designed to do harm to Ms. Jones' character and reputation. However, it is quite another matter to take a polygraph examination that will test whether one is truthful or untruthful." When evergreen, superstar pitcher Roger Clemens found his name featured in Senator Mitchell's report, he angrily denied the implication, and he told Mike Wallace, host of "60 Minutes," he might take a polygraph test to prove his innocence (but later recanted).

Polygraph evidence has a following not only among sports icons but also among politicians, celebrities, and business leaders. Disgraced Enron CEO Jeff Skilling publicized a favorable polygraph test to buttress his assertion that he had played no role in the shady dealings that led to the apocalyptic collapse of the energy giant and wiped out the retirement savings of thousands of employees. A cousin of J. K. Rowling took a lie detector test, broadcast on American television, to prove (in vain) that he had inspired the Potter character in her Harry Potter novels. Larry Sinclair, a Minnesota man who claimed to have shared a bed with then presidential candidate Barack Obama, infamously failed a polygraph challenge sponsored by Whitehouse.com. Larry Flynt introduced polygraph evidence to show that a New Orleans prostitute was telling the truth when she revealed having an extramarital affair with Senator David Vitter.

It may therefore be a surprise to find out that U.S. courts of law have long considered polygraphs inadmissible as evidence, ever since Marston attempted to set the precedent and failed in the 1920s. The standard has been loosened slightly in recent years in selected jurisdictions. Yet lawyers continue to seize headlines with lie detection results. One reason is that the public appears to trust polygraphs. The popular sentiment was underscored by the unpredicted success of the game show "The Moment of Truth," in which contestants chained to polygraph machines were dealt embarrassing questions about personal relationships, petty crimes, and sundry private matters. In a notable episode, the audience applauded as the wife of a New York police officer publicly admitted to infidelity, a statement confirmed as true by the polygraph. After debuting on Fox in January 2008, the show ended the season as the most watched new show on network television, averaging 14.6 million viewers. Jose Canseco reportedly threw his cap in the ring to face the examiner on the popular show in his unyielding quest for credibility (though such a show was never aired).

~ # # # ~

The enthusiastic, widespread usage of lie detectors runs counter to their unaccredited status in the American legal system. In the 1920s, the courts introduced a litmus test of "general acceptance," which excluded evidence from polygraphs unless and until the science attained sufficient validation. Almost a century came and went with anemic progress: the scientific community has periodically reviewed available research and repeatedly warned the public that polygraphs make too many errors to be reliable, particularly when used to screen people. Comprehensive reports in 2002 and 1983 were barely distinguishable in their executive findings. Meanwhile, legislators sent mixed messages on the issue: Congress passed the Employee Polygraph Protection Act of 1988, prohibiting American companies from conducting polygraph screening tests on potential or current employees, but it has not restrained government agencies or the police. And in 2008, Congress took a pass on scrutinizing the PCASS (Preliminary Credibility Assessment Screening System) after learning the portable lie detector was to be deployed in Iraq and Afghanistan.

Despite the lack of judicial or scientific standing, the FBI, the CIA, and the vast majority of local police forces routinely use polygraphs in criminal investigations. They utilize lie detectors indirectly, as a means to coerce suspects into making confessions. T. V. O'Malley, president of the American Polygraph Association, has compared a polygraph examination to "confessing to a priest: you feel a little better by getting rid of your baggage." Confession evidence holds awesome power in the courtroom; a noted legal scholar believes it "makes the other aspects of a trial superfluous." For this reason, federal and local law enforcement officers regard the polygraph as "the most effective collection tool in their arsenal of security tools." In the United States, it is legal to obtain confessions via the reporting of false evidence, which means the police are free to tell a suspect he or she failed a lie detector test no matter what happened.

When the U.S. Army approved PCASS in 2007, the portable gadget was intended for security screening (of non-U.S. citizens), rather than targeted investigations. This use is not new; at least ten government entities, including the FBI, the CIA, the National Security Agency, the Secret Service, the Department of Energy, the Drug Enforcement Agency, and the Defense Intelligence Agency, as well as most police forces use lie detectors to screen new or current employees. At its peak, the Department of Energy's screening program covered all twenty thousand employees; bowing to pressure from scientists and Congress, the department later cut the list to twenty-three hundred targets who have access to certain "high-risk" programs.

The polygraph's practitioners and supporters argue that the machine is accurate enough, and certainly more accurate than any alternative. They are convinced that the mere presence of the lie detector intimidates some subjects into telling the truth. Since the real deal is the confession evidence, they don't think accuracy matters as much as the academics say it does. Furthermore, polygraph results have broken open some very difficult cases.

~ *# # #* ~

A case in point was the Angela Correa murder in Peekskill, New York. On November 15, 1989, Angela strolled into the woods of Hillcrest Park to snap photographs for school. She never walked out of the park. Two days later, her partially naked body was found, covered in leaves, raped, beaten, strangled, and murdered. She was fifteen years old. We reserve the word *evil* for people who commit such heinous crimes. The police detectives, working quickly, obtained an offender profile from the New York Police Department: they were told to look for a white or Hispanic man, younger than twenty-five and probably under nineteen, shorter than five feet ten inches; someone with a physical handicap or mental slowness; a loner unsure around women but who knew Angela; someone not involved in school activities and with a history of assault, drugs, and alcohol.

From the first week, the detectives did not doubt that a classmate of Angela's had killed her. They had their eyes on sixteen-year-old Jeffrey Deskovic, who fit the NYPD profile of an introverted, young murderer, and they never looked back. Deskovic was said to have been absent from school at the time of Angela's death. Later, he showed unusual curiosity in the case, even volunteering to be interviewed by detectives without the presence of family, a friend, or a lawyer.

However, the investigation was stalling, not least because the scientific evidence proved wanting—completely negative. None of the three hair samples collected from Angela's body came from

Deskovic (the police surmised they came from the medical examiner and his assistant). No fingerprint of Deskovic's was detected on a cassette player and tape, bottles, twigs, and other items retrieved near her body. Most exasperating to the police, the DNA in the live sperm swabbed from inside her body did not match Deskovic's and instead specifically excluded him. Nor did the detectives have direct-witness testimony.

Deskovic was interviewed no fewer than seven times during the two-month investigation. He started to act as if he were part of the investigation team, sharing notes with the detectives and drawing maps of the crime scene. The police knew they had the right guy but were frustrated they had scant evidence against him.

So it was the polygraph that saved the day. On January 25, 1990, Deskovic agreed to take a polygraph exam to prove he was telling the truth. Before this day, he had steadfastly maintained his innocence. Early in the morning, he was driven to Brewster, New York, where he was cooped up for eight hours in a ten-foot by ten-foot room, facing in turns Detective McIntyre and Investigator Stephens, who played good cop, bad cop. Eventually, Stephens told Deskovic he had failed the polygraph exam, whereupon a final confrontation ensued in which Deskovic made a confession to McIntyre.

On December 7, 1990, a jury convicted Jeffrey Deskovic of murder in the second degree, rape in the first degree, and criminal possession of a weapon in the fourth degree. On January 18, 1991, he was sent to jail with a sentence of fifteen years to life. The court described it as a "classical tragedy." Deskovic ultimately served sixteen years in prison; he was released in September 2006.

Investigator Stephens, like many police officers, regarded the polygraph as a prop to "get the confession." Whereas most courts do not admit polygraph evidence, introducing a suspect's admission of guilt greatly aids a prosecutor's case; researchers have found a conviction rate of about 80 percent among U.S. criminal cases with confession evidence. In the Angela Correa case, Deskovic's confession helped the prosecutors overcome the absence of scientific evidence and witness testimony. Without the polygraph exam, there would have been no confession and thus no conviction.

~ # # # ~

In Pittsburgh, Carnegie Mellon University statistician Stephen Fienberg listened in disbelief as an MSNBC journalist spoke to him about the newly revealed PCASS, the portable lie detector. The army had already poured over $2.5 million into its development and purchased about a hundred units for troops in Iraq and Afghanistan. Professor Fienberg saw this as utter disdain for the considered opinion of American scientists on the unreliability of lie detection technologies, and of polygraphs in particular. In 2002, he had served as the technical director of the report in which the National Academy of Sciences (NAS) resoundingly rejected the polygraph as an inadequate science, especially for use in national-security screening. The key sentence of the entire report was this one:

> *Given [the polygraph's] level of accuracy, achieving a high probability of identifying individuals who pose major security risks in a population with a very low proportion of such individuals would require setting the test to be so sensitive that* hundreds, or even thousands, of innocent individuals would be implicated for every major security violator correctly identified.

This ratio of false positives to true positives (hundreds or thousands to one) elegantly captures what the scientists have dubbed the "unacceptable trade-off," which is a variant of the conundrum faced by anti-doping scientists hoping to pick out drug cheats from squads of clean athletes. Here, polygraph examiners must set the sensitivity of their machines so as to balance the benefits of possibly identifying suspicious individuals with the costs of falsely implicating law-abiding citizens. However, different settings merely redistribute errors between false positives and false negatives, not unlike using different thresholds in the hematocrit test. Addressing the flip side of this trade-off, the NAS opined, "The only way to be certain to limit the frequency of false positives is to administer the test in a manner that would almost certainly severely limit the proportion of serious transgressors identified." This science is dismal: as false positives ebb, so false negatives flow.

The 2002 NAS report specifically recommended that the government reduce or rescind the use of polygraphs for employee screening. Yet the investigative reporter from MSNBC unearthed declassified documents disclosing how the army had been aggressively pursuing a new portable polygraph gadget destined for screening use. As a knockoff of the traditional polygraph, PCASS records fewer measurements and is surely less accurate than its model. The crucial role of the examiner is abrogated, replaced by an "objective" computer program that is easily fooled by countermeasures it cannot see, such as breath control and tongue biting. What's more, NAS criticized the Johns Hopkins University lab hired to supply the computer program for being "unresponsive" to repeated requests for technical details, so that the research committee could not complete an independent evaluation of the lab's methodology. Among the uninspiring body of research on the accuracy of PCASS, most studies were conducted by the same people who developed the device itself (conflict of interest, anyone?), and none attempted to replicate the battlefield conditions under which it would be deployed. Despite the lack of serious science to back up the claims of efficacy, Congress has failed to call any hearing on PCASS.

In an act of self-regulation, the army acknowledged the weaknesses of the portable lie detector and proactively restricted its use to screening job applicants at military bases and screening potential insurgents at bomb scenes. As counterintelligence team leader David Thompson explained, the "Reds" (subjects determined to be deceptive) would face follow-on interrogations, most likely via the traditional polygraph examination, rather than immediate consequences. Implicit in this change of policy is the idea that the polygraph will be more acceptable if we set lower expectations—if we let PCASS do half the job. Such a compromise seemed as though it should please the skeptical scientific community: while the decision didn't completely shelve deployment of the flawed technology, the army at least curtailed its role.

Far from being satisfied, Fienberg's panel concluded that while polygraphs are marginally useful for targeted investigations, they are essentially worthless for screening. Alas, against lowered expectations, lie detectors perform even worse! A sports commentator would say the team is playing down to the standard of the opponent. To understand why this must be so, compare the following two situations in which the polygraph attains the 90 percent accuracy level claimed by its supporters:

Situation A: Screening
The agency believes 10 spies lurk among its 10,000 employees
   (1 in 1,000).
Of the 10 spies, the polygraph correctly identifies 90 percent
   (9) and passes 1 erroneously.
Of the remaining 9,990 good employees, the polygraph
   erroneously fails 10 percent, or 999.
For every spy caught, 111 good employees are falsely accused.

Situation B: Police Lineup
The police seek 20 murderers out of 100 suspects (1 in 5).
Of the 20 murderers, the polygraph correctly identifies 90
   percent (18) and passes 2 erroneously.
Of the remaining 80 innocent suspects, the polygraph
   erroneously fails 10 percent, or 8.
For every 9 murderers caught, 4 innocent citizens are falsely
   accused.

Notice that Situation B offers a dramatically more favorable cost-to-benefit ratio than Situation A: when the lie detector is used in a specific investigation, such as a police lineup, the price of catching each criminal is less than 1 false accusation, but when it is used for screening, the comparable cost is 111 innocents sacrificed.

Given identical accuracy levels in both situations, the real reason for this difference is the divergent ratio of criminals to innocents subject to the tests. Situation A (screening) is more trying because the presence of so many innocents (999 out of 1,000) turns even a small error rate into a bounty of false positives and a roster of ruined careers. The baseball players' union would not be pleased as Mike Lowell's worst-case scenario materialized. For security screening, one expects that almost everyone examined is neither a spy nor an insurgent, so the situation is like A, not B. To overcome the challenge of Situation A, we must have a wholly accurate technology, one that yields an exceedingly small quarry of false positives. Scientists warn against PCASS precisely because the military intends to use the gadget for screening masses of mostly innocent people; in this arena, sometimes known as "prediction of rare events," the polygraph and its variants are decidedly not Magic Lassos.

~ # # # ~

When Jeffrey Deskovic walked out of jail on September 20, 2006, he walked out a free man. He also walked out an *innocent* man. Not a typo. Deskovic became a poster boy for the Innocence Project, a pro bono legal aid consultancy dedicated to overturning wrongful convictions through the latest DNA technology. Earlier that year, the project leaders had convinced Janet DiFiore, the new Westchester County district attorney, to reexamine Deskovic's DNA. The result confirmed the original forensic finding that the quiet classmate of Angela Correa had nothing whatsoever to do with her murder. More significantly, the murderer's DNA matched Steven Cunningham, whose profile was inserted into a data bank of criminals due to a separate murder conviction for which he was serving a twenty-year sentence. Cunningham later admitted to Angela's murder and rape, closing the loop for DiFiore's office.

It took Deskovic sixteen long years to win back his freedom and innocence. At the time of his release in 2006, he was thirty-three years old but just beginning his adult life. A reporter from the *New York Times* found him struggling with the basics of modern living, such as job hunting, balancing a checkbook, driving a car, and making friends. He said, "I lost all my friends. My family has become strangers to me. There was a woman who I wanted to marry at the time I was convicted, and I lost that too."

"He had been incarcerated half his life for a crime he did not commit." DiFiore's office did not mince words in a candid review of the Angela Correa murder case. Her report continued, "Deskovic's January 25th statement was far and away the most important evidence at the trial. Without it, the State had no case against him. He would never have been prosecuted for killing Correa. He would never have been convicted. He would never have spent a day—let alone sixteen years—in prison."

Recall what transpired on that fateful day: Deskovic consented to a polygraph interrogation, during which he confessed to a crime he did not commit. The detectives concluded that Deskovic lied when he claimed innocence, and this error of judgment caused the grave miscarriage of justice. In hindsight, Deskovic was incarcerated half his life due to a false-positive error in a polygraph exam.

In a surprising twist, DiFiore acknowledged that the tactics used by the police were in fact lawful. They are allowed to seek polygraph exams (suspects may refuse) and to elicit confessions, even by citing false evidence, such as a fictitious failed polygraph result. According to Saul Kassin, a leading forensic psychologist, such investigative methods frequently produce false confessions. Up to a quarter of the convicts exonerated by the Innocence Project had admitted to crimes they did not commit, and like Jeffrey Deskovic, many had done so during polygraphs.

One might think normal people do not make false confessions. But important research by Kassin and other psychologists has refuted this sensible assumption. Kassin has said pointedly that it is innocence itself that puts innocent people at risk. The statistics show that innocent people are more likely to waive the rights designed to protect them, such as the right to silence and to counsel, and they are more likely to agree to polygraphs, house searches, and other discretionary actions. Their desire to cooperate is fueled by another "confession myth" identified by Kassin, the incorrect belief that prosecutors, judges, or jurors will know a false confession in light of other evidence (or lack thereof). Sadly, confession evidence can be overpowering. Kassin reported that in his experiments with mock juries, even when the jurors stated that they fully discounted the confession as unreliable, the conviction rates of these cases were still significantly above those of the same cases presented without the confession evidence. Furthermore, this result held even when the jurors were specifically instructed to disregard the confession.

Kassin's number one confession myth is the misconception that trained interviewers can detect truth and deception, a direct challenge to polygraph supporters. He cited studies from around the world that have consistently found that the self-anointed experts, such as police interrogators, judges, psychiatrists, customs inspectors, and the like, do no better at discerning lies than untrained eyes. More alarmingly, there is emerging evidence that professional training in interrogation techniques does not affect accuracy but merely bolsters self-confidence—a misguided conviction, if not a delusion.

The Deskovic tragedy was a case in point. Everything other than his confession was either exculpatory or erroneous. The original scientific and forensic evidence, not just the DNA test, exonerated Deskovic but was explained away by speculative theories and then ignored by the jury. For instance, the prosecution claimed that the hair samples, which were not linked to Deskovic, could have come from the medical examiner and his assistant, and the jury accepted that explanation without proof. When Deskovic maintained his innocence through the sentencing phase and beyond, asserting that he "didn't do anything," the jury chose to believe his earlier, unrecorded confession. The NYPD profile, which purportedly fit Deskovic almost perfectly, missed the mark on all fronts: the real perpetrator, Cunningham, was black, not white or Hispanic; his age was almost thirty, not under nineteen or twenty-five; and he was a complete stranger to the victim, not somebody she knew.

The psychologists worry that we are only seeing the tip of the iceberg of wrongful convictions. Statisticians elaborate: when we deploy polygraphs for screening, like those in the PCASS project, there will be *hundreds, or even thousands, of false positives for every major security threat correctly identified*. Some, perhaps most, of these will lead to false confessions and wrongful convictions.

~ # # # ~

In calibrating the computer algorithm of PCASS, the army requested that Greens (those judged to be truthful) be minimized and Reds (deceptive) be favored against Yellows (inconclusive). Accordingly, the Johns Hopkins researchers set the passing rate—that is, the percentage of Greens—at less than 50 percent. This situation is as if the anti-doping agency set the hematocrit threshold at 46 percent, thus disqualifying half of the clean athletes while ensuring that all dopers are caught. The way PCASS is calibrated tells us that army leaders are worried sick about the false negative. They are reluctant to pass any job applicant unless they can be sure the person has not lied. This policy is entirely consistent with the prevalent belief that even one undetected insurgent could prove devastating. After all, some terrorist strikes, like the anthrax attacks of 2001, can be perpetrated by a criminal acting alone, as far as we know.

By focusing its energy on making sure no potential insurgent goes unnoticed, the army is certain to have made loads of false-positive errors. Stemming from the unavoidable trade-off between the two errors, this result is clear unless one believes that the majority of the applicant pool (those judged to be Reds) could consist of insurgents. The sway of the asymmetric works in reverse relative to the case of steroid testing: here, the false-negative error can become highly toxic and highly public, while false-positive mistakes are well hidden and may come to light only through the painstaking work of activists like the Innocence Project.

~### ~

The asymmetric costs associated with national-security screening sways examiners toward condoning false positives while minimizing false negatives, which has profound consequences for all citizens. It took Jeffrey Deskovic sixteen years of perseverance, plus a pinch of good luck with the new district attorney, to expose the grave false-positive error. In several recent high-profile cases of alleged espionage, the suspects, such as the Chinese-American scientist Dr. Wen Ho Lee, reportedly flunked polygraph exams but were ultimately cleared of spying, winning multimillion-dollar settlements for their troubles. These false alarms not only cost investigators time and money in chasing dead-end leads but also tarnished the reputations and destroyed the careers of the victims and frequently also their associates. Statistical analysis confirms that many more Deskovics, perhaps hundreds or thousands a year, are out there, most likely hapless.

Even if we trust the accuracy level claimed by the Johns Hopkins researchers, we can conclude that for every true insurgent caught by PCASS, 93 regular folks would be falsely classified as deceptive, their apparent "crime" being at the wrong place at the wrong time (see Figure 4-2). The statistics largely mirror those of the earlier Situation A, in which even a tiny false-positive rate will be magnified by the presence of a large number of regular folks within the applicant pool (9,990 out of 10,000 in our example).

Figure 4-2 How PCASS Produces 100 False Alarms for Every Insurgent Caught

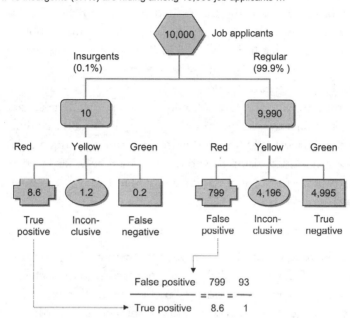

If 10 insurgents (0.1%) are hiding among 10,000 job applicants ...

In order to minimize false negatives (insurgents judged "Green"), PCASS is calibrated with a passing rate lower than 50%. Accuracy of PCASS taken from Harris and McQuarrie's study.

The portable lie detector exacts a high cost for catching the 8 or 9 insurgents, with almost 800 innocents mistaken as deceptive.

This ominous cost-to-benefit ratio ought to frighten us in four ways. First, it embodies a morbid calculus in which a crowd of almost 100 gets rounded up in response to 1 person's infraction, invoking unwelcome memories of the collective-accountability system. Second, among the Reds, there is no way of separating the 8 or 9 truly deceptive from the 800 falsely accused. Third, it makes a mockery of a "screening" device when it passes only about half of the subjects (4,995 out of 10,000) while calling most of the rest "inconclusive"; since we expect only 10 insurgents in the applicant pool, almost all of these Yellows are in fact harmless people. Fourth, there is still the unfinished business of the 1 insurgent incorrectly given the green or yellow light while almost 800 innocents see "red" haphazardly. Add to these problems the overstated accuracy level and the possibility of countermeasures, and we have one highly suspect technology.

How many innocent lives should we ruin in the name of national security? This was the question Professor Fienberg raised when he warned against PCASS and other lie detection techniques. "It may be harmless if television fails to discriminate between science and science fiction, but it is dangerous when government does not know the difference."

~ # # # ~

Truth be told, detection systems are far from perfect. Steroid testing suffers from a bout of false-negative errors, so drug cheats like Marion Jones and many others can hide behind strings of negatives. It is one thing to look for known molecular structures inside test tubes; it is quite another thing to vet the words of suspected liars. As Jose Canseco realized, the polygraph is one of few instruments our society trusts in these situations. However, statisticians say lie detectors produce excessive false-positive errors that result in false accusations, coerced confessions, dead-end leads, or ruined lives; the cruel fate visited upon Jeffrey Deskovic and undoubtedly numerous others serves to warn us against such excesses. Worse, the accuracy of detection systems slips markedly when the targets to be detected occur rarely or are measured indirectly; this explains why preemployment screening for *potential* security threats is harder than screening for *past* security violations through indirect physiological measures, which is harder than detecting a specific steroid molecule.

In the meantime, the public discourse is focused on other matters. In steroid testing, we keep hearing about the false-positive problem—how star athletes are being hunted by supercilious testers. In national security, we fear the false negative—how the one terrorist could sneak past the screening. As a result, the powers that be have decided that falsely accusing athletes and failing to detect terrorists are more expensive than undetected drug cheats and wrongful convictions.

Statisticians tell us to evaluate both types of errors at the same time, because they are interconnected through an unavoidable trade-off. In practice, the two errors often carry asymmetric costs, and in calibrating detection systems, decision makers, knowingly or not, will be swayed by the error that is public and toxic. For drug tests, this is the false positive, and for polygraphs, it is the false negative. But the trade-off ensures that any effort to minimize this error will aggravate the other; and because the other error is less visible, its deterioration is usually unnoticed.

Short of a technological breakthrough that dramatically improves the overall accuracy of polygraphs, it is not possible to reduce false positives and false negatives simultaneously, leaving us with an unacceptable, unpleasant trade-off. This trade-off is as true in PCASS as in other large-scale screening initiatives, including various data-mining constructs rumored to have sprouted in the "War on Terror."

After September 11, 2001, a vast new market opened up for data-mining software, previously purchased primarily by large businesses. It is generally accepted that the terrorist attacks could have been prevented if our intelligence agencies had only "connected the dots" "in time." Thus, by building gigantic databases that keep tabs on everyone—storing all phone calls, e-mails, websites visited, bank transactions, tax records, and so on—and by unleashing search agents, spiders, bots, and other exotically named software species to sift through the data at lightning speeds—shaking out patterns and tendencies—our government can uncover plots before the terrorists strike. These secretive, expansive programs go by creative monikers such as TIA (Total Information Awareness; later renamed Terrorism Information Awareness), ADVISE (that's Analysis, Dissemination, Visualization, Insight, and Semantic Enhancement), and Talon (apparently not an acronym). A celebratory confidence pervades the data-mining community as they make bold promises, as in the following example from Craig Norris, CEO of Attensity, a Palo Alto, California–based start-up that counts the National Security Agency and Department of Homeland Security as customers: "You don't even have to know what it is you're searching for. But you'll know it once you find it. If a terrorist is planning a bombing, they might say, 'Let's have a barbecue.' The software can detect if the word *barbecue* is being used more often than usual."

If only real life were so perfect.

Using data-mining software to find terrorist plots is comparable to using polygraphs for preemployment screening in that we collect information about past or current behavior in order to predict future misconduct. In either case, reliance on indirect evidence and the sway of false negatives relative to false positives tend to produce lots of false alarms. Moreover, both applications involve prediction of rare events, and terrorist plots are even rarer than spies! Rarity is measured by how many relevant objects (say, spies) exist among the total pool of objects (say, employees). As every detail of our daily lives is sucked into those gigantic databases, the number of objects examined swells at a breakneck pace, while the number of known terrorist plots does not. Therefore, relevant objects become rarer and harder to find. If data-mining systems perform as accurately as polygraphs, they will drown under the weight of false positives in less time than it takes to sink PCASS.

Security expert Bruce Schneier has looked at data-mining systems the same way we evaluated steroid tests and polygraphs:

"We'll assume the [data-mining] system has a one in 100 false-positive rate . . . and a one in 1,000 false-negative rate. Assume one trillion possible indicators to sift through: that's about 10 events—emails, phone calls, purchases, web destinations, whatever—per person in the United States per day. Also assume that 10 of them are actually terrorists plotting. This unrealistically accurate system will generate one billion false alarms for every real terrorist plot it uncovers. *Every day of every year, the police will have to investigate 27 million potential plots in order to find the one real terrorist plot per month. Raise that false-positive accuracy to an absurd 99.9999 percent and you're still chasing 2,750 false alarms per day but that will inevitably raise your false negatives, and you're going to miss some of those 10 real plots."*

But a realistic data-mining system does not surpass the accuracy level of polygraphs, so Schneier's numbers (diagrammed in Figure 4-3) are wildly optimistic, as he admonished.

Statisticians who perform the type of exploratory analysis Norris described, in which the computer discovers you-know-it-once-you-see-it patterns, know such findings are only approximate. To appropriate Norris's example, if no prior terrorist has ever used *barbecue* as a code word, no data-mining system will tag it as suspicious. If there were such a prescient system, it would throw off millions of false alarms (*picnic, umbrella, beach, sneakers*, etc.). We would then have to inaugurate a new class of crime, excessive communal verbal redundancy, to describe the dangerous state of repeating a word or a phrase too many times on one's own or within one's social network.

Figure 4-3 How Data-Mining Technologies Produce Billions of False Alarms

If 10 terrorist-related objects are hidden among 1 trillion objects …

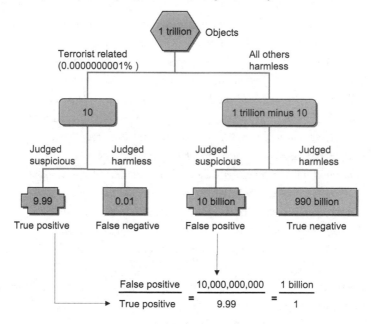

Because of the number of harmless objects being examined, even a tiny false positive rate results in a huge number of errors. Accuracy of data-mining technology taken from Schneier's highly optimistic scenario.

Expecting intelligence agencies to "connect the dots" is a pipe dream. Which dots mattered revealed themselves only after 9/11. The idea that we knew the dots and only needed someone to join them was classic 20/20 hindsight. Imagine: if trains rather than planes had been involved, we would now be fidgeting about other dots!

The endless drumbeat about the miracle of data-mining systems tells us we have drawn the wrong lessons from 9/11. Sure, the tragedy made tangible the unimaginable cost of a false-negative mistake, of failing to identify potential terrorists. But too much fear of false negatives has inevitably resulted in too many false positives. It therefore makes statistical sense that few Guantanamo inmates have been convicted and many detainees were declared innocent or released without charge. When marketers use data mining to guess which customers will respond positively to sale offers, false positives may cause selected customers to receive junk mail; when banks use data mining to guess which credit card transactions may be fraudulent, false positives may cost honest customers time to call and verify blocked charges. These are inconveniences when compared with the psychological trauma and shattered lives that could stem from a charge of "excessive communal verbal redundancy." Apart from false imprisonment and loss of civil liberties, we must also consider how demoralizing, how expensive, and how counterproductive it is for our intelligence agents to be chasing down millions of bad leads.

What we should have learned from 9/11 is that terrorist plots are extremely rare events. Existing detection technologies are not accurate enough to qualify for the job; we know polygraphs can't do it, and large-scale data-mining systems perform even worse. The unacceptable trade-off remains just as unacceptable. The Magic Lasso is still elusive. We need something much, much better.

5

Jet Crashes / Jackpots

The Power of Being Impossible

*The safest part of your journey is over. Now drive
home safely.*

—ANONYMOUS PILOT

*1,000,000,000,000,000,000,000,000,000,000,
000,000,000,000,000,000*

—A QUINDECILLION

On August 24, 2001, a store clerk in Ontario, Canada, claimed a CDN$250,000 prize in the Encore lottery. On October 31, 1999, a Boeing 767 jetliner plunged into the Atlantic Ocean off Nantucket Island, Massachusetts, leaving no survivors. On the surface, these two events—winning a fortune and losing everything—had nothing to do with each other. Except when one considers how improbable either of these events was. Statisticians who keep score tell us that the odds of winning the Encore lottery are one in ten million, roughly comparable to the odds of dying in a plane crash. At these long odds, practically none of us will live long enough to win the Encore lottery or to perish in a plane crash. Yet about 50 percent of Americans play the state lotteries, and at least 30 percent fear flying. Our belief in miracles underlies both these attitudes: even if rare events do not happen often, when they do happen, they will happen to us. If someone's ticket is going to win the million-dollar jackpot, it will be ours, so we gamble. If a plane is going to vanish in the Atlantic, it will be the one taking us, so we avoid flying.

By contrast, statisticians typically take the contrary view: they write off the chance of jackpots and are not worried about jet crashes. Why would they expose themselves to the risk of death but exclude themselves from the dream of riches? Can they be serious?

~ # # # ~

It was almost 2:00 A.M., on October 31, 1999—the Sunday morning of a Halloween weekend, long after the residents of the pristine Nantucket Island had waved off their reveling friends on an unseasonably cool night. Stuart Flegg, a carpenter who had moved to a southeastern cliff of Nantucket eleven years before, was lounging in his backyard with buddies and beers, under the stars. Without warning, an orange fireball growled in the night sky and then faded quietly into the darkness. Stuart rubbed his eyes, as if to check his state of mind, and poked his friend on the back, pointing in the direction of the flash. It was unlike anything he had ever seen. Stuart and his friends prattled on for a bit, and then they let the thread drop.

Word seemed to come out of nowhere and creep through the neighborhood like wild vines. A few minutes before, from thirty-three thousand feet above sea level, a Boeing 767 jet had cut out a sixty-six-degree angle as it split and nose-dove, scattering 217 souls in the azure Atlantic waters. The horrified passengers on board EgyptAir Flight 990 had endured a precipitous fall at four hundred feet per second, followed by an abrupt surge up eight thousand feet, only to tumble again, this time in finality. Many more details would trickle out over the coming months and years. At this time and place, to those witnesses, to the relatives of the perished, and their friends and neighbors, the impact was head-on and devastating.

Recognition of the disaster quickly gave way to disbelief, then to scant hope; soon information brought about acceptance of the tragic and an outpouring of sadness. With little delay, curiosity set in as well, in the form of loving concern: *Do I know anyone scheduled to fly tonight? From Boston Logan? On EgyptAir? Heading to Cairo?* A single no brought relief, while four yeses brought fear, denial, and busy fingers on a cell phone. For most, the fear of losing a loved one would come and go, though uncertainty would linger, now in the form of foresight: *Better to cancel business trips and vacations for the near future. Better to travel on land than by air. Better to shun those dangerous foreign airlines. Better to avoid Logan, or night flights, or layovers in JFK. Never again save a penny.*

~ # # # ~

Ninety miles away in Boston, the newsrooms buzzed to life. By midmorning, CBS, NBC, Fox, ABC, CNN, MSNBC, and Fox News had all swapped out their regular programming to carry continuous coverage of The Crash. Few businesses thrive on the morbid as much as the media, particularly on sleepy weekends bereft of ready-made headlines. Journalists on the disaster beat knew this was their time to shine. For the next week, if not the entire month, their reports would land on the front page and stay in the public's conscience. The extent of the media coverage is reflected in the statistics of *New York Times* front-page stories: researchers found 138 articles for every 1,000 plane crash deaths, but only 2 articles for every 1,000 homicides, and only 0.02 article for every 1,000 cancer deaths.

The Sunday of the crash, the front pages of newspapers big and small announced the air disaster with absolute solemnity. Sorting through the headlines, one might recognize the five prototypal disaster beat stories: the tragedy narrative about the available facts of the case; the human interest story singling out one unfortunate victim; the feel-good story about communities pulling together to cope with the disaster; the detective report citing analyses from all angles, from engineers, insurers, passersby, psychologists, and even psychics; and the big-picture synthesis, courtesy of the editors.

The editorial piece has a predictable structure, frequently referencing a list of recent air tragedies, compiled in a table similar to this one:

Corridor of Conspiracy

Year	Date	Location	Flight	Deaths
1996	Jul 17	Long Island, N.Y.	TWA 800	230
1998	Sept 2	Nova Scotia, Canada	Swissair 111	229
1999	Jul 16	Martha's Vineyard, Mass.	JFK Jr.'s flight	3
1999	Oct 31	Nantucket, Mass.	EgyptAir 990	217

Presented with such a table, we look for patterns of occurrence. *Seek and ye shall find*—that is a law of statistics. It doesn't take a genius, or a news editor, to notice that between 1996 and 1999, a succession of jets plunged into the Atlantic near Nantucket: TWA, Swissair, EgyptAir, and John F. Kennedy Jr.'s private plane. Speaking to an Associated Press reporter, a local diving instructor lamented, "Nantucket is like the Bermuda Triangle of the Northeast." He was not the only one making that connection. Many reporters also connected the dots, so to speak.

Rounding out the piece, the editors would cite the latest polls confirming the heightened level of worry about air travel. Then they would advise readers to remain calm, reminding them that experts still consider flying to be safe relative to other forms of transportation.

The editorial stance on the EgyptAir disaster was predictable, and so was the lukewarm reaction to its call for calm. It is common during such times that emotions clash against logic, superstition against science, faith against reason. Hovering in the air was the obvious question: what had caused EgyptAir 990 to crash? The journalists were running at full tilt, consulting any and all experts, whose theories more often than not conflicted with each other. No chain of logic was denied, as one report after another flooded the news. The more information provided to the public, the greater confusion it caused, and the more speculation it created. Starting with the rational explanations, such as equipment failure or atmospheric anomaly, suspicion shifted to the sinister, such as terrorist attack or drunken pilot, and then to the bizarre, like electromagnetic interference, missile attack, or pilot suicide. Finally, logical reasoning gave way to raw emotion. Unable to point the finger at a specific airline, airport, jet manufacturer, or day of the week, the public turned its back on the concept of flying altogether. Many travelers canceled or postponed their planned trips, while others opted to jump into their cars instead. Fully half the people polled by *Newsweek* after the EgyptAir crash said they experienced fear when flying, and about the same proportion indicated they would avoid airlines from Egypt and other Middle Eastern countries. Wary of its stigma, the airline quietly retired the flight's number. This fog of emotions would not clear for a few years, which is how long it takes for official air traffic accident investigations to conclude.

Taking a self-imposed moratorium on air travel is not much different from performing the rain dance to fight off a severe drought or beating drums to scare off locusts. When reason is exhausted, emotions fill up the void. But experience should teach us that logical reasoning bears the best hope, even in the face of inexplicable calamity. During the locust outbreak of 2004, African leaders convened and resolved to employ drums—the kind that hold pesticide.

At this point, you may be expecting a gotcha about misunderstanding relative risk, but we will not go there. If a lot of people come to the same conclusion about something, there must be a certain logic behind it. Interviews with people who said they would stop flying after hearing about a major crash showed that their anxiety was deeply felt. They understood that plane crashes were exceptionally rare; after all, only a handful of fatal accidents hit the developed world during the 1990s. But people feared that these accidents were more likely to occur on their flights than on others. They were asking, if air crashes were random, what could explain the unlikely coincidence of four fatal accidents in four years occurring in the same air space? They felt sure the morbid record was a conspiracy of the unknown: though nobody had yet identified the culprit, they knew something must have caused the crash. They thought the pattern was too tidy to have been the dirty work of random chance. In 1999, many were blaming the "Bermuda Triangle" over Nantucket.

While such allegations sound outlandish, the line of reasoning behind them reflects sound statistical thinking. Based on the pattern of occurrence, these folks rejected the idea that air crashes happened at random; instead, they believed in some sort of pre-determination (Bermuda Triangle, equipment failure, drunken pilot, and the like). Statisticians call this logic "statistical testing," and we use it all the time, often without knowing.

If that is so, then why do the experts get so worked up over people's fears after any plane crash? In 2001, Professor Arnold Barnett, the nation's foremost airline safety expert, dared to ask rhetorically, "Is aviation safety . . . a problem that has been essentially solved [in the First World], to the extent that talking about it might suggest a personality disorder?" In even starker terms, Professor Barry Glassner, a psychologist who wrote *The Culture of Fear*, reckoned that the hysteria after a plane crash is as deadly as the crash itself because people who abandon their flight plans face a greater risk of dying—from road accidents. Why did these experts look at the same list of fatalities but come to the opposite conclusion? How could they explain the coincidence of four crashes in four years in the same general area? More importantly, how could they continue to trust foreign airlines?

~ # # # ~

On August 24, 2001, the Ontario Lottery and Gaming Corporation (OLG) awarded a CDN$250,000 check to Phyllis and Scott LaPlante, lucky winners of the Encore lottery on July 13, 2001. Each CDN$1 Encore ticket bought a chance to win CDN$250,000 if all six digits matched. With the odds of winning listed as one in ten million, someone who spends CDN$1 on Encore every day can expect to win once every twenty-seven thousand years, which rounds to about . . . never. Barnett, the air safety expert, has estimated that the chance of dying from a plane crash on a U.S. domestic nonstop flight is also one in ten million. Someone who takes one such flight every day would live twenty-seven thousand years before encountering a fatal crash. Thus, either event has about the same microscopic chance of happening.

What made Phyllis LaPlante's case special was her insider status: she and her husband owned Coby Milk and Variety, a small store in Coboconk, Ontario, which sold, among other things, lottery tickets. When she scanned the winning ticket, the machine chimed twice, announcing a major win. As her prize money exceeded CDN$50,000, it triggered an "insider win" investigation. Tracing the trail of tickets, the OLG staff cleverly deduced that the winner stuck to a regular set of numbers (9 4 2 9 8 1) in every lottery. So they asked for some old tickets, and the LaPlantes duly provided a few. The numbers matched.

What had actually taken place was that Phyllis LaPlante had just robbed an eighty-two-year-old man of a quarter of a million dollars. It took a statistician to prove the case decisively—using the logic of statistical testing—and determine if LaPlante was simply lucky or mighty crafty. In addressing this question, Jeffrey Rosenthal at the University of Toronto examined seven years of draws and winners of Ontario jackpots. Between 1999 and 2005, there were 5,713 "major" winners of prizes valued at CDN$50,000 or more. Rosenthal estimated that store owners and employees accounted for about CDN$22 million of the CDN$2.2 billion spent on Ontario lotteries during this period—that is to say, about CDN$1 out of every CDN$100 the OLG received. He reasoned that if store owners and employees were no luckier than everyone else, they would have won 1 out of every 100 major prizes, meaning about 57 of the 5,713 wins. But as shown in Figure 5-1, by the time Rosenthal completed his count, store insiders had actually struck gold more than 200 times! Either we had to believe that LaPlante and other store owners were blessed with extraordinary luck, or we might suspect foul play. Rosenthal was convinced of the latter.

"The fifth estate," a television program of the Canadian Broadcasting Corporation (CBC), broke the scandal on October 25, 2006, when it told the story of Bob Edmonds, the eighty-two-year-old senior citizen and bona fide winner of that Encore lottery. The winning numbers were a combination of birthdays: his own, his wife's, and his son's. The CBC hired Rosenthal to be the expert witness. He announced that the odds of lottery store insiders taking 200 of the OLG's 5,713 major prizes *by luck alone* were one in a quindecillion. (That's the number 1 followed by forty-eight zeros.) No reasonable person could believe in such luck. On the strength of Rosenthal's statistical analysis, the sorry story expanded beyond Phyllis LaPlante; up to 140 store insider wins now appeared highly dubious, and complaints deluged the OLG.

Figure 5-1 Expected Wins Versus Actual Wins by Retailer Insiders, 1999–2005: Evidence of Foul Play

	Expected wins	Actual wins
Retail insiders	57	200

You may be wondering just how the LaPlantes produced those old lottery tickets matching Edmonds's regular numbers. It was an old-fashioned con game, preying on a genial old man. When Bob Edmonds handed his ticket to the clerk on his lucky day, the scanning machine buzzed twice, indicating a big win. Distrusting his own ears, Edmonds instead believed LaPlante when she told him he had won the lesser prize of a free ticket. When LaPlante reported her "win" to OLG, she was clued in about the automatic insider-win investigation. The next day, her husband called Edmonds to the store, and they peppered him with questions. They learned that the winning numbers were his regular numbers and even obtained some of Edmonds's old losing tickets. Edmonds probably did not think expired, losing tickets would be valuable to anyone. He thought he was friends with the clerks at the corner store, but he was wrong. In an interview, he even suggested LaPlante might have been coming on to him that day! He was definitely wrong there. He realized his mistakes when the local newspaper reported that the LaPlantes were lucky winners of the Encore lottery, and he immediately filed a complaint with OLG, which eventually led to the CBC's investigation.

The story had a happy ending, though. The investigation by "the fifth estate" unleashed a maelstrom of controversy. Ontario's premier, Dalton McGuinty, was particularly alarmed because in Canada, proceeds from lotteries support the provincial budgets. In Ontario, this sum amounted to CDN$650 million in 2003–2004. About CDN$30 out of every CDN$100 spent on lotteries makes its way to the government coffers (while only CDN$54 out of every CDN$100 is paid out in prize money, ensuring that on average, the house always wins handily). A collapse in public trust in these lotteries could seriously affect Ontario's health care, education, and infrastructure. Therefore, McGuinty directed the provincial ombudsman to investigate the OLG's handling of complaints from customers. Put on the defensive, the OLG belatedly apologized to and recompensed Edmonds, released him from a prior gag order, and announced tighter regulations on insider players. The LaPlantes were sued for fraud but settled out of court after surrendering CDN$150,000 to Edmonds.

~ # # # ~

Upon analyzing the lottery win data, Rosenthal uncovered an unusual pattern of wins by retail store insiders, much too unusual to have been produced by chance. With similar logic, some people stopped flying after the EgyptAir crash because to them, four crashes in four years seemed like an unusual pattern of disasters in the same region—too many to have happened completely at random. Did such behavior constitute a "personality disorder"?

The facts on the ground were immutable: the four flights, the location, the accident times, and the number of casualties were there for all to see. Many rejected random chance as an explanation for the pattern of crashes. Yet, to Professor Barnett, four in four looked just like the work of chance. He even used the same tool of statistical testing but arrived at a different conclusion. The difference lay in how he assimilated the data.

Statisticians are a curious lot: when given a vertical set of numbers, they like to look sideways. They look into the nooks and crannies; they look underneath the cracks; they turn over every pebble. From decades of experience, they learn that what is hidden is just as important as what is in front of their eyes. No one ever gets to see the whole picture, so the key is to *know what you don't know.* When you read the table of fatalities presented earlier, you may have visualized four black dots over the "Nantucket Triangle" and connected the dots; Barnett, by contrast, saw four black dots plus millions of white dots. Each white dot stood for one flight that safely traversed the air space during those four years. Seen in this light, we would hardly find the black dots, let alone connect them. Then, taking it further,

Barnett envisioned ten, even twenty, years of flights over the Nantucket Triangle, bringing millions more white dots into the picture, and only dozens of additional black dots. This method creates a new picture, one altogether different from the list of worst disasters frequently displayed in postcrash news reports. Listed separately, the four accidents stuck out like stars in the night sky; however, they became all but invisible when buried within a sea of whiteness (see Figure 5-2). Considering that the Northeast Corridor is one of the busiest airways in the world, it would follow that this area would see a larger number of fatal accidents.

As to whether fear of flying could be considered a "personality disorder," one esteemed statistician answered firmly in the negative during a lecture to an audience at Boeing. He suggested that as the airline industry has fended off systematic causes of jet crashes such as equipment failure, new types of risks are rising to the surface. He cited three "menaces that caused scant fatalities in the 1990s but which could cause more deaths in forthcoming years": sabotage, runway collisions, and midair collisions. The lecture, titled "Airline Safety: End of a Golden Age?" could not have been more aptly timed; it was delivered on September 11, 2001. The future he had anticipated arrived early.

Figure 5-2 The Statistician's Worldview

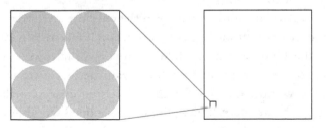

Four accidents
separately

Four accidents in
context, not to scale

Who was this professor with such impressive foresight? None other than Arnold Barnett, who has been studying airline safety data for more than thirty years at the MIT Sloan School of Management. In the 1970s, he initiated a remarkably productive research program that has continuously tracked the safety record of airlines worldwide. Before he arrived on the scene, people considered it impossible to measure airline safety accurately, because the contributing factors could not be directly observed. How could one appraise the attitudes of corporate managers toward safety? How could one compare the efficacy of different training programs? How could one take into account disparate flight routes, airports, flight lengths, and age of airlines? Barnett the statistician made an end run around these obstacles, realizing he did not need any of those unknowns. When a passenger boards a plane, his or her fear is solely of dying in a fatal crash; it is thus sufficient to merely track the frequency of fatal accidents and the subsequent survival rates. Similarly, universities rely on SAT scores and school ranks to evaluate applicants because they cannot possibly visit every family, every home, and every school. How to compare Mary's parents to Julia's? How to rank Michael's gymnasium against Joseph's? So, instead of measuring such specific influences on student achievement as parental upbringing and quality of education, educators merely track the actual scholastic ability as represented by SAT scores and school ranks.

Under Barnett's watch, airlines in the developed world saw the risk of death drop from 1 in 700,000 in the 1960s to 1 in 10 million in the 1990s, a fourteen-fold improvement in three decades. He was the first to prove that American carriers were the safest in the world, and by 1990, he was telling everyone about a golden age of air safety. The rest of the developed world has since caught up, while the developing world still lags by two decades. Barnett believes that fatal air crashes have essentially become random events with a minuscule strike rate. In other words, it is no longer possible to find any systematic cause of an air disaster, like mechanical failure or turbulence. Air crashes today are practically freak accidents.

What does the visionary Barnett say about two of our biggest fears?

1. **Don't choose between U.S. national airlines based on safety.** Jet crashes occur randomly, so the carrier that suffers a recent crash would have been merely unlucky. Between 1987 and 1996, USAir happened to be the unlucky airline. It operated 20 percent of domestic flights but accounted for 50 percent of all crash fatalities, by far the worst record among the seven major airlines in the United States (see Figure 5-3). Barnett asked what the chance was that such a lopsided allocation of deaths could have hit any one of the seven carriers. The chance was 11 percent; it was quite likely to happen, and if not USAir, another airline would have borne the brunt. In another study, Barnett found that no U.S. airline has sustained an advantage in safety: the top-ranked airline in one period frequently came in last in the next period, giving further proof that all operators were materially equal in safety. It is just not possible to predict which airline will suffer the next fatal crash. Passengers have nowhere to run for air safety.

Figure 5-3 Relative Proportion of Flights and Deaths for USAir and Six Other U.S. Carriers, 1987–1996: Evidence That USAir Was Less Safe?

	Flights	Deaths
USAir	20%	50%
Other U.S. carriers	80%	50%

2. **Don't avoid foreign airlines, even after one of their planes has crashed.** Flights operated by developing-world airlines are just as safe as those run by U.S. airlines on routes where they directly compete with one another, typically those between the developed and developing worlds. Where they do not overlap, foreign airlines suffer many more crashes, for unknown reasons. (Some speculate that they may be assigning better crews to international flights.) Because of their poor domestic record, the overall risk of death associated with developing-world carriers was eight times worse than for their developed-world peers. But Barnett found no difference between these two groups of operators on competing routes: the risk was about 1 in 1.5 million during 2000–2005. The once-a-day frequent flier could expect to die in a jet crash in 4,100 years, on any of the operators that offer service on these routes. Moreover, while the worldwide risk of aviation fatality has been more than halved since the 1980s, the risk differential between developing-world and developed-world operators has stayed minute. Thus, we can trust these supposedly hulking, inefficient state enterprises with old planes, undertrained pilots, and unmotivated staff to take us overseas safely.

Like Rosenthal, Barnett used statistical testing to prove his point. For the decade leading up to 1996, developing-world airlines oper-

Figure 5-4 Relative Proportion of Flights and Deaths for Developed-World and Developing-World Carriers, 1987–1996: No Evidence That Developing-World Carriers Were Less Safe on Comparable Routes

	Flights	Deaths
Developed-world carriers	38%	45%
Developing-world carriers	62%	55%

ated 62 percent of competitive flights. If they were just as safe as U.S. airlines, they should have caused about 62 percent of passenger deaths, or well over 62 percent if they were more prone to disasters. In those ten years, developing-world carriers caused only 55 percent of the fatalities, indicating that they did no worse (see Figure 5-4).

~ # # # ~

The news about the Ontario lottery investigation spread all over Canada, and in every province, the lottery corporations were overrun by phone calls and e-mails from concerned citizens.

British Columbia's ombudsman, in reviewing past winners, unmasked dozens of extraordinarily lucky store owners, including one who took home CDN$300,000 over five years, winning eleven times. When the president of the British Columbia Lottery Corporation, which runs the province's lottery, was fired, his buddy, himself a former president, came to his defense: "Of course, it's possible retailers cheated players of their prize money, but only if you're a fool."

In New Brunswick, the Atlantic Lottery Corporation, which runs lotteries in four provinces, attempted to reshape the publicity by hiring an external consultant to audit past wins using the same method as Rosenthal. The analysis, however, showed that between 2001 and 2006, store owners claimed 37 out of 1,293 prizes of CDN$25,000 or more, when they were expected to have won fewer than 4 of those. It was inconceivable that this group of players could have won so many prizes if each ticket had an equal chance of winning.

Meanwhile, the CBC hired Rosenthal again, this time to examine the pattern of wins in the lotteries in the Western provinces from November 2003 to October 2006. The professor found that insiders earned sixty-seven wins of CDN$10,000 or more—

twice as many as could be expected if the lotteries were fair to all players. Just how lucky were these insiders? Using statistical testing, Rosenthal further explained that the chance was 1 in 2.3 million that insiders could have racked up so many wins under a fair lottery system. While not as extreme as in Ontario, these odds were still negligible. Again, Rosenthal could hardly believe that the store owners were that much luckier than the rest of the ticket holders, so he suspected fraud. (Unlike in Ontario, neither the Atlantic nor the Western Lottery Corporation has been able to catch any individual cheater.)

To restore the public's confidence, the lottery authorities announced a series of measures to protect customers, including installation of self-service scanning machines, reconfiguration of monitors to face out to the customers, improvement in win-tracking technology, background checks for retailers, and the requirement of winners to sign the back of their winning tickets. It remains to be seen whether these policies will succeed at lifting the cloud of suspicion.

~ # # # ~

Both statisticians grappled with real-life data, noticed unusual patterns, and asked whether they could occur by chance. Rosenthal's answer was an unequivocal no, and his result raised myriad doubts about insider wins in Ontario lotteries. Employing the same type of logic, Barnett alleviated our fear of flying by showing why air travelers have nowhere to run, because freak accidents can hit any unlucky carrier, anywhere.

You may still be wondering why statisticians willingly accept the risk of death while they show little appetite for playing with chance. Why do they behave differently from most people? We know it is not the tools at their disposal that affect their behavior; we all use the same sort of statistical testing to weigh the situational evidence against chance, whether we realize it or not. The first difference lies in the way that statisticians perceive data: most people tend to hone in on unexpected patterns, but statisticians like to evaluate these against the background. For Barnett, the background is the complete flight schedule, not just a list of the worst disasters, while for Rosenthal, it includes all lottery players, not just retailers with major wins.

Moreover, in the worldview of statisticians, *rare is impossible:* jackpots are for dreamers, and jet crashes for paranoids. For Rosenthal to believe that all retail store insiders acted with honor, he would have had to accept that an extremely rare event had taken place. That would require disavowing his statistical roots. Barnett keeps on flying, twice a week, as he believes air disasters are nigh extinct. Had he stopped out of fear at any point, he would have had to admit that an incredibly unlikely incident could occur. That, too, would contravene his statistical instinct.

Rather than failing at risk assessment, as many have alleged, the people who avoid flying after air crashes also are reasoning like statisticians. Faced with a raft of recent fatal crashes, they rule out the possibility of chance. What leads them to draw different conclusions is the limited slice of data available to them. There are many everyday situations in which we run statistical tests without realizing it. The first time our bags get searched at the airport, we might rue our luck. If it happens twice, we might start to wonder about the odds of being picked again. Three or four times, and we might seriously doubt whether selection has been random at all. Rare is impossible.

~ # # # ~

At the request of two senators in 1996, the Federal Aviation Administration acted to close the information gap between the experts and the public by releasing limited air safety data on its website. How have we done since? Poorly, unfortunately. As of 2006, anyone can find black dots (the disasters) in those databases but not the white dots (the safe arrivals). Every incident from total loss to no damage is recorded with ample details, making it difficult to focus on the relevant events. Clearly, weak execution has run afoul of good intention. It is time we started turning over those pebbles! As the professors showed us, a few well-chosen numbers paint a far richer picture than hundreds of thousands of disorganized data.

Conclusion

"Statistical thinking is hard," the Nobel prize winner Daniel Kahneman told a gathering of mathematicians in New York City in 2009. A revered figure in the world of behavioral economics, Professor Kahneman spoke about his renewed interest in this topic, which he first broached in the 1970s with his frequent collaborator Amos Tversky. The subject matter is not inherently difficult, but our brains are wired in such a way that it requires a conscious effort to switch away from the default mode of reasoning, which is not statistical. Psychologists found that when research subjects were properly trained, and if they recognized the statistical nature of the task at hand, they were much likelier to make the correct judgment.

Statistical thinking is distinct from everyday thinking. It is a skill that is learned. What better way to master it than to look at positive examples of what others have accomplished. Although they rarely make the headlines, many applied scientists routinely use statistical thinking on the job. The stories in this book demonstrate how these practitioners make smart decisions and how their work benefits society.

In concluding, I review the five aspects of statistical thinking:

1. The discontent of being averaged: *Always ask about variability.*
2. The virtue of being wrong: *Pick useful over true.*
3. The dilemma of being together: *Compare like with like.*
4. The sway of being asymmetric: *Heed the give-and-take of two errors.*
5. The power of being impossible: *Don't believe what is too rare to be true.*

Some technical language is introduced in these pages; it can be used as guideposts for those wanting to explore the domain of statistical thinking further. The interstitial sections called "Crossovers" take another look at the same stories, the second time around revealing another aspect of statistical thinking.

The Discontent of Being Averaged

Averages are like sleeping pills: they put you in a state of stupor, and if you overdose, they may kill you.

That must have been how the investors in Bernie Madoff's hedge fund felt in 2008, when they learned the ugly truth about the streak of stable monthly returns they'd been receiving up until then. In the dream world they took as real, each month was an average month; variability was conquered—nothing to worry about. Greed was the root cause of their financial ruin. Those who doubted the absence of variability in the reported returns could have saved themselves; instead, most placed blind faith in the average.

The overuse of averages pervades our society. In the business world, the popular notion of an annualized growth metric, also called "compound annual growth rate," is borne from erasing all year-to-year variations. A company that is expanding at 5 percent per year *every year* has the same annualized growth rate as one that is growing at 5 percent per year *on average* but operates in a volatile market so that the actual growth can range from 15 percent in one year to −10 percent in another. The financing requirements of these two businesses cannot be more different. While the compound annual growth rate provides a useful basic summary of the past, it conveys a false sense of stability when used to estimate the future. The statistical average simply carries no information about variability.

Statistical thinking begins with noticing and understanding variability. What gets commuters upset? Not the average travel time to work, to which they can adjust. They complain about unexpected delays, occasioned by unpredictable accidents and weather emergencies. Such variability leads to uncertainty, which creates anxiety. Julie Cross, the Minnesota commuter in Chapter 1, was surely not the only driver who found "picking the fastest route" to be "a daily gamble."

It is therefore no surprise that effective measures to control congestion attack the problem of variability. For Disney guests arriving during busy hours, FastPass lines eliminate the uncertainty of waiting time by spacing out spikes in demand. Similarly, metered ramps on highways regulate the inflow of traffic, promising commuters smoother trips once they enter.

The Disney "Imagineers" and the highway engineers demonstrated impressive skills in putting theoretical science into practice. Their seminal achievements were in emphasizing the behavioral aspect of decision making. The Disney scientists learned to focus their attention on reducing perceived wait times, as distinct from actual wait times. In advocating perception management, they subordinated the well-established research program in *queuing theory*, a branch of applied mathematics that has produced a set of sophisticated tools for minimizing actual average wait times in queues. As with traditional economics, queuing theory makes an assumption about rational human behavior that does not match reality. For example, in putting up signs showing inflated estimates of waiting time, the Disney engineers counted on irrationality, and customer surveys consistently confirmed their judgment. For further exploration of the irrational mind, see the seminal work of Daniel Kahneman, starting with his 2003 overview article "Maps of Bounded Rationality: Psychology for Behavioral Economics" in *American Economic Review*, and *Predictably Irrational* by Dan Ariely.

Political considerations often intrude on the work of applied scientists. For instance, Minnesota state senator Dick Day seized upon the highway congestion issue to score easy points with his constituents, some of whom blamed the ramp-metering policy for prolonging their commute times. A huge commotion ensued, at the end of which the highway engineers were vindicated. The Minnesota Department of Transportation and the senator agreed to a compromise solution, making small changes to how the meters were operated. For applied scientists, this episode conveyed the valuable lesson that the technical good (reducing actual travel time) need not agree with the social good (managing the public's perception). Before the "meters shutoff" experiment, engineers doggedly pursued the goal of delaying the onset of congestion, which preserves the carrying capacity of highways and sustains traffic flow. The experiment verified the technical merit of this policy: the benefits of smoother traffic on the highway outweighed the drawback of waiting at on-ramps. Nevertheless, commuters disliked having to sit and stew at the ramps even more than they disliked the stop-and-go traffic on jam-packed highways.

Statisticians run *experiments* to collect data in a systematic way to help make better decisions. In the Minnesota experiment, the consultants performed a form of *pre–post analysis*. They measured traffic flow, trip time, and other metrics at preselected sections of the highways before the experiment and again at its conclusion. Any difference between the pre- period and post- period was attributed to shutting off the ramp meters.

But note that there is a hidden assumption of "all else being equal." The analysts were at the mercy of what they did not, or could not, know: was all else really equal? For this reason, statisticians take absolute caution in interpreting pre–post studies, especially when opining on why the difference was observed during the experiment. The book *Statistics for Experimenters* by George Box, Stuart Hunter, and Bill Hunter is the classic reference for proper design and analysis of experiments. (The Minnesota experiment could have benefited from more sophisticated statistical expertise.)

Crossovers

Insurance is a smart way to exploit variability, in this case, the ebb and flow of claims filed by customers. If all policyholders required payout concurrently, their total losses would swallow the cumulative surplus collected from premiums, rendering insurers insolvent. By combining a large number of risks acting independently, actuaries can reliably predict average future losses and thus set annual premiums so as to avoid financial ruin. This classic theory works well for automotive insurance but applies poorly to catastrophe insurance, as Tampa businessman Bill Poe painfully discovered.

For auto insurers, the level of total claims is relatively stable from year to year, even though individual claims are dispersed over time. By contrast, catastrophe insurance is a "negative black swan" business, to follow Nassim Taleb's terminology. In Taleb's view, business managers can be lulled into ignoring certain extremely unlikely events ("black swans") just because of the remote chance of occurrence, even though the rare events have the ability to destroy their businesses. Hurricane insurers hum along merrily, racking up healthy profits, until the big one ravages the Atlantic coast, something that has little chance of happening but wreaks extreme damage when it does happen. A mega-hurricane could cause $100 billion in losses—fifty to a hundred times higher than the damage from the normal storm. The classic theory of insurance, which invokes the bell curve, breaks down at this point because of extreme variability and severe spatial concentration of this risk. When the black swan appears, a large portion of customers makes claims simultaneously, overwhelming insurers. These firms might still be solvent *on average*—meaning that over the long run, their premiums would cover all claims—but the moment cash balances turn negative, they implode. Indeed, catastrophe insurers who fail to plan for the variability of claims invariably find themselves watching in horror as one ill wind razes their entire surplus.

Statisticians not only notice variability but also recognize its type. The more moderate type of variability forms the foundation of the automotive insurance business, while the extreme type threatens the hurricane insurers. This is why the government "take-out" policy, in which the state of Florida subsidizes entrepreneurs to take over policies from failed insurers, made no sense; the concentrated risks and thin capital bases of these start-up firms render them singularly vulnerable to extreme events.

~###~

Variability is the reason why a steroid test can never be perfectly accurate. When the International Cycling Union (UCI), the governing body for cycling, instituted the hematocrit test as a makeshift method for catching EPO dopers, it did not designate a positive finding as a doping violation; rather, it set a threshold of 50 percent as the legally permissible hematocrit level for participation in the sport. This decision reflected UCI's desire to ameliorate the effect of any false-positive errors, at the expense of letting some dopers escape detection. If all normal men were to have red blood cells amounting to precisely 46 percent of their blood volume (and all dopers were to exceed 50 percent), then a perfect test can be devised, marking up all samples with hematocrit levels over 46 percent as positive, and those below 46 percent as negative. In reality, it is the proverbial "average male" who comes in at 46 percent; the "normal" hematocrit level for men varies from 42 to 50 percent. This variability complicates the tester's job: someone with red cell density of, say, 52 percent can be a blood doper but can also be a "natural high," such as a highlander who, by virtue of habitat, has a higher hematocrit level than normal.

UCI has since instituted a proper urine test for EPO, the hormone abused by some endurance athletes to enhance the circulation of oxygen in their blood. Synthetic EPO, typically harvested from ovary cells of Chinese hamsters, is prescribed to treat anemia induced by kidney failure or cancer. (Researchers noted a portion of the annual sales of EPO could not be attributed to proper clinical use.) Because EPO is also naturally secreted by the kidneys, testers must distinguish between "natural highs" and "doping highs." Utilizing a technique known as isoelectric focusing, the urine test establishes the acidity profiles of EPO and its synthetic version, which are known to be different. Samples with a basic area percentage (BAP), an inverse measure of acidity, exceeding 80 percent were declared positive, and these results were attributed to illegal doping (see Figure C-1).

To minimize false-positive errors, timid testers set the threshold BAP to pass virtually all clean samples including "natural highs," which had the effect of also passing some "doping highs." This led Danish physician Rasmus Damsgaard to assert that many EPO-positive urine samples were idling in World Anti-Doping Agency (WADA) labs, their illicit contents undetected. If testers would lower the threshold, more dopers would get caught, but a few clean athletes would be falsely accused of doping. This trade-off is as undesirable as it is unavoidable. The inevitability stems from variability between urine samples: the wider the range of BAP, the harder it is to draw a line between natural and doping highs.

Figure C-1 Drawing a Line Between Natural and Doping Highs

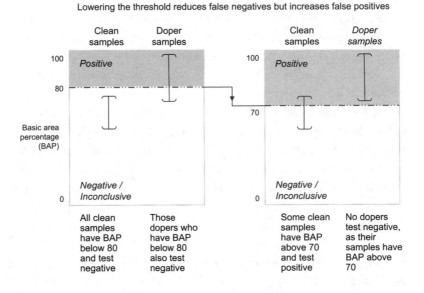

Lowering the threshold reduces false negatives but increases false positives

| Clean samples | Doper samples | | Clean samples | Doper samples |

All clean samples have BAP below 80 and test negative

Those dopers who have BAP below 80 also test negative

Some clean samples have BAP above 70 and test positive

No dopers test negative, as their samples have BAP above 70

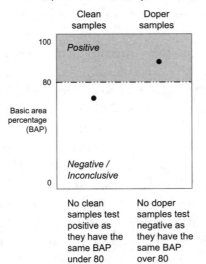

When samples have no variability, the test can be perfect

No clean samples test positive as they have the same BAP under 80

No doper samples test negative as they have the same BAP over 80

Because the anti-doping laboratories face bad publicity for false positives (while false negatives are invisible unless the dopers confess), they calibrate the tests to minimize false accusations, which allows some athletes to get away with doping.

The Virtue of Being Wrong

The subject matter of statistics is variability, and *statistical models* are tools that examine why things vary. A disease outbreak model links causes to effects to tell us why some people fall ill while others do not; a credit-scoring model identifies correlated traits to describe which borrowers are likely to default on their loans and which will not. These two examples represent two valid modes of statistical modeling.

George Box is justly celebrated for his remark "All models are false but some are useful." The mark of great statisticians is their confidence in the face of fallibility. They recognize that no one can have a monopoly on the truth, which is unknowable as long as there is uncertainty in the world. But imperfect information does not intimidate them; they seek models that fit the available evidence more tightly than all alternatives. Box's writings on his experiences in the industry have inspired generations of statisticians; to get a flavor of his engaging style, see the collection *Improving Almost Anything*, lovingly produced by his former students.

More ink than necessary has been spilled on the dichotomy between correlation and causation. Asking for the umpteenth time whether correlation implies causation is pointless (we already know it does not). The question *Can correlation be useful without causation?* is much more worthy of exploration. Forgetting what the textbooks say, most practitioners believe the answer is quite often yes. In the case of credit scoring, correlation-based statistical models have been wildly successful even though they do not yield simple explanations for why one customer is a worse credit risk than another. The parallel development of this type of model by researchers in numerous fields, such as pattern recognition, machine learning, knowledge discovery, and data mining, also confirms its practical value.

In explaining how credit scoring works, statisticians emphasize the similarity between traditional and modern methods; much of the criticism leveled at credit-scoring technology applies equally to credit officers who make underwriting decisions by handcrafted rules. Credit scores and rules of thumb both rely on information from credit reports, such as outstanding account balances and past payment behavior, and such materials contain inaccurate data independently of the method of analysis. Typically, any rule discovered by the computer is a rule the credit officer would also use if he or she knew about it. While the complaints from consumer advocates seem reasonable, no one has yet proposed alternatives that can overcome the problems common to both systems. Statisticians prefer the credit-scoring approach because computers are much more efficient than loan officers at generating scoring rules, the resulting rules are more complex and more precise, and they can be applied uniformly to all loan applicants, ensuring fairness. Industry leaders concur, pointing out that the advent of credit scoring precipitated an explosion in consumer credit, which boosted consumer spending, hoisting up the U.S. economy for decades. Consider this: since the 1970s, credit granted to American consumers has exploded by 1,200 percent, while the deep recession that began in 2008 has led to retrenchment at less than 10 percent a year.

Statistical models do not relieve business managers of their responsibility to make prudent decisions. The credit-scoring algorithms make educated guesses on how likely each applicant will be to default on a loan but shed no light on how much risk an enterprise should shoulder. Two businesses with different appetites for risk will make different decisions, even if they use the same credit-scoring system.

When correlation is not enough to be useful without causation, the stakes get dramatically higher. Disease detectives must set their sights on the source of contaminated foods, as it is irresponsible to order food recalls, which cripple industries, based solely on evidence of correlation. The bagged spinach case of 2006 revealed the sophistication required to solve such a riddle. The epidemiologists used state-of-the-art statistical tools like the case–control study and information-sharing networks; because they respect the limits of these methods, they solicited help from laboratory and field personnel as well.

The case also demonstrated the formidable challenges of outbreak investigations: urgency mounted as more people reported sick, and key decisions had to be made under much uncertainty. In the bagged-spinach investigation, every piece of the puzzle fell neatly into place, allowing the complete causal path to be traced, from the infested farm to the infected stool. Investigators were incredibly lucky to capture the P227A lot code and discover the specific shift when the contamination had occurred. Many other investigations are less than perfect, and mistakes not uncommon. For example, a Taco Bell outbreak in November 2006 was initially linked to green onions but later blamed on iceberg lettuce. In 2008, when the Food and Drug Administration (FDA) claimed tomatoes had caused a nationwide salmonella outbreak, stores and restaurants immediately yanked tomatoes from their offerings, only to discover later that they had been victims of a false alarm. Good statisticians are not daunted by these occasional failures. They understand the virtue in being wrong, as no model can be perfect; they particularly savor those days when everything works out, when we wonder how they manage to squeeze so much out of so little in such a short time.

Crossovers

Disney fans who use Len Testa's touring plans pack in an amazing number of attractions during their visits to Disney theme parks, about 70 percent more than the typical tourist; they also shave off three and a half hours of waiting time and are among the most gratified of Disney guests. In putting together these plans, Testa's team took advantage of correlations. Most of us realize that many factors influence wait times at a theme park, such as weather, holiday, time of the day, day of the week, crowd level, popularity of the ride, and early-entry mornings. Similar to credit-scoring technology, Testa's algorithm computed the relative importance of these factors. He told us that the popularity of rides and time of day matter the most (both rated 10), followed by crowd level (9), holiday (8), early-entry morning (5), day of week (2), and weather (1). Thus, in terms of total waiting time, there really was no such thing as an off-peak day or a bad-weather day. How did Testa know so much?

Testa embraced what epidemiologists proudly called "shoe leather," or a lot of walking. On any brilliant summer day in Orlando, Florida, Testa could be spotted among the jumpy 8:00 A.M. crowd at the gates of Walt Disney World, his ankles taped up and toes greased, psyched up for the rope drop. The entire day, he would be shuttling between rides. He would get neither in line nor on any ride; every half hour, upon finishing one loop, he would start over at the first ride. He would walk for nine hours, logging eighteen miles. To cover even more ground, he had a small staff take turns with different rides, all year round. In this way, they collected wait times at every ride every thirty minutes. Back at the office, the computers scanned for patterns.

Testa's model did not attempt to explain why certain times of the day were busier than others; it was enough to know which times to avoid. As interesting as it would be to know how each step of a touring plan decreased their wait times, Testa's millions of fans care about only one thing: whether the plan let them visit more rides, enhancing the value of their entry tickets. The legion of satisfied readers is testimony to the usefulness of this correlational model.

~ # # # ~

Polygraphs rely strictly on correlations between the act of lying and certain physiological metrics. Are correlations useful without causation? In this case, statisticians say no. To avoid falsely imprisoning innocent people based solely on evidence of correlation, they insist that lie detection technology adopt causal modeling of the type practiced in epidemiology. They caution against logical overreach: *Liars breathe faster. Adam's breaths quickened. Therefore, Adam was a liar.* Deception, or stress related to it, is only one of many possible causes for the increase in breathing rate, so variations in this or similar measures need not imply lying. As with epidemiologists studying spinach and *E. coli*, law enforcement officials must find corroborative evidence to strengthen their case, something rarely accomplished. A noteworthy finding of the 2002 NAS report was that scientific research into the causes of physiological changes associated with lying has not kept up with the spread of polygraphs. The distinguished review panel on the report underlined the need for coherent psychological theories that explain the connection between lying and various physiological measures.

For the same reason, data-mining models for detecting terrorists are both false and useless. Data-mining models uncover patterns of correlation. Statisticians tell us that rounding up suspects based on these models will inevitably ensnare hundreds or thousands of innocent citizens. Linking cause to effect requires a much more sophisticated, multidisciplinary approach, one that emphasizes shoe leather, otherwise known as human intelligence gathering.

The Dilemma of Being Together

In 2007, the average college-bound senior scored 502 in the Critical Reading (verbal) section of the SAT. In addition, girls performed just as well as boys (502 and 504, respectively), so nothing was lost by reporting the overall average score, and a bit of simplicity was gained. The same could not be said of blacks and whites, however, as the average black student tallied 433, almost 100 points below the average white student's score of 527. To aggregate or not to aggregate: that is the dilemma of being together. Should statisticians reveal several group averages or one overall average?

The rule of thumb is to keep groups together if they are alike and to set them apart if they are dissimilar. In our example, after the hurricane disasters of 2004–2005, insurers in Florida reassessed the risk exposure of coastal residents, deciding that the difference relative to inland properties had widened so drastically that the insurers could no longer justify keeping both groups together in an undifferentiated risk pool. Doing so would have been wildly unfair to the inland residents.

The issue of *group differences* is at the heart of the dilemma. When group differences exist, groups should be disaggregated. It is a small tragedy to have at our disposal ready-made groups to partition people into, such as racial groups, income groups, and geographical groups. This easy categorization conditions in us a cavalier attitude toward forming comparisons between blacks and whites, the rich and the poor, red and blue states, and so on. Statisticians tell us to examine such group differences carefully, as they frequently cover up nuances that break the general rule. For instance, the widely held notion that the rich vote Republican fell apart in a review of state-by-state data. Andrew Gelman, a statistician at Columbia University, found that this group difference in voting behavior surfaced in "poor" states like Mississippi but not in "rich" states like Connecticut. (See his fascinating book *Red State, Blue State, Rich State, Poor State* for more on this topic.) Similarly, the Golden Rule settlement failed because the procedure for screening out unfair test items lumped together students with divergent ability levels. The mix of ability levels among black students varied from that among whites, so this rule produced many false alarms, flagging questions as unfair even when they were not.

Statisticians regard this as an instance of the famous *Simpson's paradox*: the simultaneous and seemingly contradictory finding that no difference exists between high-ability blacks and high-ability whites; no difference exists between low-ability blacks and low-ability whites; and when both ability levels are combined, blacks fare significantly worse than whites. To our amazement, the act of aggregation manufactures an apparent racial gap!

Here is what one would expect: since the group differences are zero for both high- and low-ability groups, the combined difference should also be zero. Here is the paradox: the statistics show that in aggregate, whites outperform blacks by 80 points (the bottom row of Figure C-2). However, the confusion dissipates upon

Figure C-2 Aggregation Creates a Difference: An Illustration of Simpson's Paradox

	Paradox			Explanation
	Score of high-ability group	Score of low-ability group	Average score	Mix of high ability to low ability
White students	600	400	520	60% : 40%
Black students	600	400	440	20% : 80%
White–Black difference	0	0	80	

Paradox: Black students of high ability score the same as whites (600); the scores for low-ability students of both races are also the same (400). And yet, the average white student score of 520 is 80 points higher than the average black student score.

Explanation: Due to superior educational resources, 60% of white students have high ability compared to only 20% of black students. Thus, the average white student score of 520 is heavily weighted by the score of high-ability students (600), while the black student score of 440 is heavily weighted by the score of low-ability students (400).

realizing that white students typically enjoy better educational resources than blacks, a fact acknowledged by the education community, so the average score for whites is more heavily weighted toward the score for high-ability students, and the average for blacks toward the score for low-ability students. In resolving the paradox, statisticians compute an average for each ability level so as to compare like with like. Simpson's paradox is a popular topic in statistics books, and it is a complicated concept at first glance.

The recognition of Simpson's paradox led to a breakthrough in fair testing. The procedure for differential item functioning (DIF) analysis, introduced in Chapter 3, divides examinees into groups of like ability and then compares average correct rates within these groups. Benefiting from research by the Educational Testing Service (ETS) in the 1980s, DIF analysis has rapidly gained acceptance as the scientific standard. In practice, ETS uses five ability groups based on total test score. For the sake of simplicity, we only concerned ourselves with the case of two groups.

The strategy of *stratification* (analyzing groups separately) is one way to create like groups for comparison. A superior alternative strategy is *randomization*, when feasible. Statisticians frequently assign test subjects randomly into one group or another; say, in a clinical trial, they will select at random some patients to be given placebos, and the remainder to receive the medicine under study. Because of random assignment, the groups will have similar characteristics: the mix of races will be the same, the mix of ages will be the same, and so on. In this way, "all else being equal" is assured when one group is chosen for special treatment. If the treatment has an effect, the researcher does not have to worry about other contributing factors. While statisticians prefer randomization to stratification, the former strategy is sometimes infeasible. For example, in DIF analysis, social norms would prevent one from exposing some students *randomly* to higher-quality schools and others to lower-quality schools.

By contrast, the attempt by Florida insurers to disaggregate the hurricane risk pools has pushed the entire industry to the brink in the late 2000s. This consequence is hardly surprising if we recall the basic principle of insurance—that participants agree to cross-subsidize each other in times of need. When the high-risk coastal policies are split off and passed to take-out companies with modest capital bases, such as Poe Financial Group, or to Citizens Property Insurance Corporation, the state-run insurer of last resort, these entities must shoulder a severe concentration of exposure, putting their very survival into serious question. In 2006, Poe became insolvent after 40 percent of its customers bled a surplus of ten years dry in just two seasons.

Crossovers

By Arnold Barnett's estimation, between 1987 and 1996, air carriers in the developing world sustained 74 percent of worldwide crash fatalities while operating only 18 percent of all flights (see Figure C-3a). If all airlines were equally safe, we would expect the developing-world carriers to share around 18 percent of fatalities. To many of us, the message could not be clearer: U.S. travelers should stick to U.S. airlines.

Yet Barnett contended that Americans gained nothing by "buying local," because developing-world carriers were just as safe as those in the developed world. He looked at the same numbers as most of us but arrived at an opposite conclusion, one rooted in the statistics of group differences. Barnett discovered that the developing-world airlines had a much better safety record on "between-worlds" routes than on other routes. Thus, lumping together all routes created the wrong impression.

Since domestic routes in most countries are dominated by home carriers, airlines compete with each other only on international routes; in other words, about the only time American travelers

Figure C-3 Stratifying Air Routes: Relative Proportion of Flights and Deaths by Developing-World and Developed-World Carriers, 1987–1996

(a) When all routes were lumped together, developing-world carriers looked worse:

	Flights	Deaths
Developing-world carriers	18%	74%
Developed-world carriers	82%	26%

(b) On routes between the two worlds, developing-world carriers weren't less safe:

	Flights	Deaths
Developing-world carriers	62%	55%
Developed-world carriers	38%	45%

get to choose a developing-world carrier is when they are flying between the two worlds. Hence, only the between-worlds routes are relevant. On these relevant routes, over the same period, developing-world carriers suffered 55 percent of the fatalities while making 62 percent of the flights (see Figure C-3b). That indicates they weren't more dangerous than developed-world airlines.

Group differences entered the picture again when comparing developed-world and developing-world carriers on between-worlds routes only. The existence of a group difference in fatality rates between the two airline groups is what would compel us to reject the equal-safety hypothesis.

Any stratification strategy should come with a big warning sign, statisticians caution. Beware the cherry-picker who draws attention only to one group out of many. If someone presented only Figure C-3b, we could miss the mediocre safety record of developing-world carriers on their domestic routes, surely something we ought to know while touring around a foreign country.

Such mischief of omission can generally be countered by asking for information on every group, whether relevant or not.

~ # # # ~

Stratification produces like groups for comparison. This procedure proved essential to the proper fairness review of questions on standardized tests. Epidemiologists have known about this idea since Sir Bradford Hill and Sir Richard Doll published their landmark 1950 study linking smoking to lung cancer, which heralded the case–control study as a viable method for comparing groups. Recall that Melissa Plantenga, the analyst in Oregon, was the first to identify the eventual culprit in the bagged-spinach case, and she based her hunch on a 450-item shotgun questionnaire, which revealed that four out of five sickened patients had consumed bagged spinach. Disease detectives cannot rely solely on what proportion of the "cases" (those patients who report sickness) were exposed to a particular food; they need a point of reference—the exposure rate of "controls" (those who are similar to the cases but not ill). A food should arouse suspicion only if the cases have a much higher exposure rate to it than do the controls. Statisticians carefully match cases and controls to rule out any known other factors that may also induce the illness in one group but not the other.

In 2005, a year before the large *E. coli* outbreak in spinach, prepackaged lettuce salad was blamed for another outbreak of *E. coli*, also of class O157:H7, in Minnesota. The investigators interviewed ten cases, with ages ranging from three to eighty-four, and recruited two to three controls, with matching age, for each case patient. In the case–control study, they determined that the odds of exposure to prepackaged lettuce salad was eight times larger for cases than for controls; other evidence subsequently confirmed this hypothesis.

The result of the study can also be expressed thus: among like people, those in the group who fell ill were much more likely to

Figure C-4 The Case–Control Study: Comparing Like with Like

Proportion exposed to . . .

	Any kind of lettuce	Prepackaged lettuce salad	Dole prepackaged lettuce salad
Case patients	90%	90%	90%
Controls	65%	38%	22%

have consumed prepackaged lettuce salad than those in the group who did not become ill (see Figure C-4). In this sense, the case–control study is a literal implementation of comparing like with like. When like groups are found to be different, statisticians will treat them separately.

The Sway of Being Asymmetric

If all terrorists use *barbecue* as a code word and we know Joe is a terrorist, then we are certain Joe also uses the word *barbecue*. Applying a general truth (all terrorists) to a specific case (Joe the terrorist) is natural; going the other way, from the specific to the general, carries much peril, and that is the playground for statisticians. If we are told Joe the terrorist says "barbecue" a lot, we cannot be sure that all other terrorists also use that word, as even one counterexample invalidates the general rule.

Therefore, when making a generalization, statisticians always attach a *margin of error*, by which they admit a chance of mistake. The inaccuracy comes in two forms: *false positives* and *false negatives*, which are (unhelpfully) called *type I* and *type II* errors in statistics texts. They are better understood as false alarms and missed opportunities. Put differently, accuracy encompasses the ability to correctly detect positives as well as the ability to correctly detect negatives. In medical parlance, the ability to detect true positives is known as *sensitivity*, and the ability to detect true negatives is called *specificity*. Unfortunately, improving one type of accuracy inevitably leads to deterioration of the other. See the textbook *Stats: Data and Models* by Richard D. De Veaux for a formal discussion under the topic of *hypothesis testing*, and the series of illuminating expositions on the medical context by Douglas Altman, published in *British Medical Journal*.

When anti-doping laboratories set the legal limit for any banned substance, they also fix the trade-off between false positives and false negatives. Similarly, when researchers configure the computer program for the PCASS portable lie detector to attain desired proportions of red, yellow, and green results, they express their tolerance of one type of error against the other. What motivates these specific modes of operation? Our discussion pays particular attention to the effect of *incentives*. This element falls under the subject of *decision theory*, an area that has experienced a burst of activity by so-called behavioral social scientists.

In most real-life situations, the costs of the two errors are unequal or *asymmetric*, with one type being highly publicized and highly toxic, and the other side going unnoticed. Such imbalance skews incentives. In steroid testing, false negatives are invisible unless the dopers confess, while false positives are invariably mocked in public. No wonder timid testers tend to underreport positives, providing inadvertent cover for many dopers. In national-security screening, false negatives could portend frightening disasters, while false positives are invisible until the authorities reverse their mistakes, and then only if the victims tell their tales. No wonder the U.S. Army configures the PCASS portable polygraph to minimize false negatives.

Not surprisingly, what holds sway with decision makers is the one error that can invite bad press. While their actions almost surely have made the other type of error worse, this effect is hidden from view and therefore neglected. Because of such incentives, we have to worry about false negatives in steroid testing and false positives in polygraph and terrorist screening. For each drug cheat caught by anti-doping labs, about ten other cheaters have escaped detection. For each terrorist trapped by polygraph screening, hundreds if not thousands of innocent citizens have been falsely implicated. These ratios are worse when the targets to be tested are rarer (and spies or terrorists are rare indeed).

The bestselling *Freakonomics* provides a marvelously readable overview of behavioral economics and incentives. The formulas for false positives and false negatives involve *conditional probabilities* and the famous *Bayes' rule*, a landmark of any introductory book on statistics or probability. For the sake of simplicity, textbook analysis often assumes the cost of each error to be the same. In practice, these costs tend to be unequal and influenced by societal goals such as fairness as well as individual characteristics such as integrity that may conflict with the objective of scientific accuracy.

Crossovers

Banks rely on credit scores to make decisions on whether to grant credit to loan applicants. Credit scores predict how likely customers are to repay their loans; arising from statistical models, the scores are subject to errors. Like polygraph examiners, loan officers have strong incentives to reduce false negatives at the expense of false positives. False-negative mistakes put money in the hands of people who will subsequently default on their loans, leading to bad debt, write-offs, or even insolvency for the banks. False-positive errors result in lost sales, as the banks deny worthy applicants who would otherwise have fulfilled their obligations. Notice, however, that false positives are invisible to the banks: once the customers have been denied loans, the banks could not know if they would have met their obligations to repay the loan or not. Unsurprising, such asymmetric costs coax loan officers into rejecting more good customers than necessary while reducing exposure to bad ones. It is no accident that these decisions are undertaken by the risk management department, rather than sales and marketing.

The incentive structure is never static; it changes with the business cycle. During the giant credit boom of the early 2000s, low interest rates pumped easy money into the economy and greased a cheap, abundant supply of loans of all types, raising the opportunity cost of false positives (missed sales). At the same time, the economic expansion lifted all boats and lessened the rate of default of the average borrower, curtailing the cost of false negatives (bad debt). Thus, bank managers were emboldened to chase higher sales at what they deemed lower risks. But there was no free lunch: dialing down false positives inevitably generated more false negatives, that is, more bad debt. Indeed, by the late 2000s, banks that had unwisely relaxed lending standards earlier in the decade sank under the weight of delinquent loans, which was a key factor that tipped the United States into recession.

~ # # # ~

Jeffrey Rosenthal applied some statistical thinking to prove that mom-and-pop store owners had defrauded Ontario's Encore lottery. Predictably, a howl of protests erupted from the accused. Leaders of the industry chimed in, too, condemning his damning report as "outrageous" and maintaining that store owners had "the highest level of integrity."

Was it a false alarm? From the statistical test, we know that if store owners had an equal chance in the lotteries as others, then the probability they could win at least 200 out of 5,713 prizes was one in a quindecillion (1 followed by forty-eight zeros), which was practically zero. Hence, Rosenthal rejected the no-fraud hypothesis as impossible. The suggestion that he had erred was tantamount to believing that the insiders had beaten the rarest of odds fair and square. The chance of this scenario occurring naturally—that is, the chance of a false alarm—would be exactly the previous probability. Thus, we are hard-pressed to doubt his conclusion.

(Recall that there is an unavoidable trade-off between false positives and false negatives. If Rosenthal chose to absorb a higher false-positive rate—as much as one in a hundred is typical—he could reduce the chance of a false negative, which is the failure to expose dishonest store owners. This explains why he could reject the no-fraud hypothesis for western Canada as well, even though the odds of 1 in 2.3 million were higher.)

The Power of Being Impossible

Statistical thinking is absolutely central to the scientific method, which requires theories to generate testable hypotheses. Statisticians have created a robust framework for judging whether there is sufficient evidence to support a given hypothesis. This framework is known as *statistical testing*, also called *hypothesis testing* or *significance testing*. See De Veaux's textbook *Stats: Data and Models* for a typically fluent introduction to this vast subject.

Take the fear of flying developing-world airlines. This anxiety is based on the hunch that air carriers in the developing world are more prone to fatal accidents than their counterparts in the developed world. Arnold Barnett turned around this hypothesis and reasoned as follows: if the two groups of carriers were equally safe, then crash fatalities during the past ten years should have been scattered randomly among the two groups in proportion to the mix of flights among them. Upon examining the flight data, Barnett did not find sufficient evidence to refute the equal-safety hypothesis.

All of Barnett's various inquiries—the comparison between developed-world and developing-world carriers, the comparison among U.S. domestic carriers—pointed to the same general result: that it was *not* impossible for these airlines to have equal safety. That was what he meant by passengers having "nowhere to run"; the next unlikely crash could befall any carrier.

Statistical tests can also lead to the other conclusion, that what happened *is* impossible. For example, Jeffrey Rosenthal demonstrated that it was impossible for store insiders to win the Encore lotteries with such frequency if one were to assume they had the same chance of winning as everyone else. The minute probability he computed, one in a quindecillion, is technically known as the *p-value* and signifies how unlikely the situation was. The smaller the p-value, the more impossible the situation, and the greater its power to refute the no-fraud scenario. Then, statisticians say, the result has *statistical significance*. Note that this is a matter of magnitude, rather than direction. If the p-value were 20 percent, then there would be a one-in-five chance of seeing at least 200 insider wins in seven years despite absence of fraud, and then Rosenthal would not have sufficient evidence to overturn the fair-lottery hypothesis. Statisticians set a minimum acceptable standard of evidence, which is a p-value of 1 percent or 5 percent. This practice originated with Sir Ronald Fisher, one of the giants of statistical thinking. For a more formal treatment of p-values and statistical significance, look up the topics of hypothesis testing and confidence intervals in a statistics textbook.

The statistical testing framework demands a disbelief in miracles. If we were not daunted by odds of one in a quindecillion, then we could believe that Phyllis LaPlante was just an incredibly, incredibly lucky woman. But then we had better believe that the next flight we take could be our last. Since statisticians are trained to think rare is impossible, they do not fear flying, and they do not play lotteries.

Crossovers

Psychometricians use the principle of statistical testing to determine the presence of DIF (differential item functioning) in a standardized test. A test item is said to have DIF if one group of examinees finds it more difficult than does another group of examinees with similar abilities. If the group difference is 1 percent, one would hesitate to conclude that the test item is unfair. However, if the gap is 15 percent, one would be likely to sound the alarm. As in the lottery analysis, the matter concerns the magnitude, not so much the direction, of the difference. Indeed, ETS policy brands significant differences in either direction as unacceptable.

In effect, the ETS researchers ask, "If the test item is fair to both groups, how rare would it be for the difference between black and white examinees to be as large as presently observed (or larger)?" They seek the answer by using actual scores from experimental sections of the SAT. In the 1980s, ETS realized that for this analysis to make sense, the examinees must first be matched on their "ability"; otherwise, ETS could not attribute any gap in performance directly to unfair item design. Statisticians say matching removes the *confounding* of the two factors, item design and quality of education. While several methods exist to measure DIF, they all make use of the framework of statistical testing.

~ # # # ~

In Minnesota, an ambitious experiment was organized to measure how turning off ramp meters on the highway entrances would affect the state of congestion. From the viewpoint of statistical testing, the doubters led by Senator Day wanted to know, if ramp metering was useless, what was the likelihood that the average trip time would rise by 22 percent (the improvement claimed by engineers who run the program) after the meters were shut off? Because this likelihood, or p-value, was small, the consultants who analyzed the experiment concluded that the favorite tool of the traffic engineers was indeed effective at reducing congestion.

Since statisticians do not believe in miracles, they avoided the alternative path, which would assert that a rare event—rather than the shutting off of ramp meters—could have produced the deterioration in travel time during the experiment. Such an event might have been a twenty-five-year snowstorm or a fifty-car pileup (neither happened). In practice, if an experiment had indeed occurred under abnormal conditions, it would yield no insight on the question under study, and a new experiment should be arranged.

Numbers Rule Your World

While reading this book, it may dawn on you that numbers of all kinds rule your world. When you drive on the highway, engineers are measuring your speed at the on- and off-ramps. If your family goes to Walt Disney World, you may notice that cameras pick up your movement between rides, or you may bump into Len Testa or his crew counting heads. You now know that credit scores don't have to make sense in order to work in your favor. But when the FDA recalls this food or that, you would want to know if the agency has located those lot codes. If you or your children have taken a standardized test, you should know how the test developers choose questions that are fair to everyone. Those living in hazard-prone areas can now see why private insurers are staying away. The next time you hear a busted athlete complain about a witch hunt by steroid testers, you may wonder about those negative samples lying around in the labs. When the next lie detection program arrives to screen out potential terrorists, you may wonder about those innocent people put behind bars by mistake. After you board a plane, you will relax, knowing that you have nowhere to run. And when you decide to play the lottery, you will look closely at the person selling you the ticket.

If you react in those ways, as I hope you do, you will be thinking like a statistician.

Perhaps now, when you next get on the Internet to pull up the stock charts, you will think about how the variability of returns should affect your investment strategy. When the FDA yanks another blockbuster drug from the market, you will ask how certain the agency had been that this drug caused patients to get better in the first place. While checking out the latest discovery of a new health supplement, you will scrutinize which groups are being compared, whether they are comparable, and whether you belong to one of them. In the supermarket, you won't be surprised when the computer issues you a seemingly nonsensical discount coupon, pitching a product you'd never use—indeed, you may ponder the relative cost of the two errors (false positive and false negative). When offered another mouth-watering investment idea, you'd want to know how tiny the chance is of sustaining stable financial returns over thirty years if you assume the fund manager is not a swindler.

If you know how to use numbers in making everyday decisions, *you* rule your world.

Notes

In these notes, I document key sources, recommend further reading, and fill in certain details that were left out of the preceding chapters. A complete bibliography is available at the book's link on my website, www.junkcharts.typepad.com.

General References

Books on statistical thinking fall into three general categories.

The popular category of "damned lies and statistics," in which authors collect insightful, uproarious examples of mischief with numbers, came into its own with Darrell Huff's *How to Lie with Statistics*, still the cream of the crop five decades after its publication. Other notable contributors include Howard Wainer, a leading industry statistician (*Graphic Discovery*, *Visual Revelations*, among others); John Allen Paulos, a tireless advocate of numerical literacy (*Innumeracy*, *A Mathematician Reads the Newspaper*, among others); and Ed Tufte, an expert in graphical presentation of information (*The Visual Display of Quantitative Information*, *Visual Explanations*, among others). My blog, called Junk Charts (www.junkcharts.typepad.com), critiques and reconstitutes graphics from the mainstream press. The science reporter Ben Goldacre debunks statistical fallacies regularly on his Bad Science blog (www.badscience.net).

The second category, history and biographies, is evergreen. For those with some training in mathematics, the two books by Stephen Stigler on the historical development of statistical thinking are indispensable. Stigler, a professor at the University of Chicago, wrote elegant essays on the "average man" and other Adolphe Quetelet discoveries. Biographies of important statisticians such as Karl Pearson and Sir Francis Galton are available. Trade books on statistics tend to emphasize its probabilistic foundations and are filled with historical or hypothetical examples and biographical sketches. Among these, Jeffrey Rosenthal's *Struck by Lightning* is short and sweet. In addition, the following more specialized books are exceptional: Stephen Senn's *Dicing with Death* focuses on applications in medical sciences; John Haigh's *Taking Chances* demystifies lotteries and games of chance; William Poundstone's *Fortune's Formula* dissects a specific gambling strategy; and Ian Ayres's *Super Crunchers* considers the use of data mining by businesses.

Finally, among textbooks, the set by Richard D. De Veaux, Paul Velleman, and David Bock (*Intro Stats, Stats: Modeling the World, Stats: Data and Models*) earns my highest recommendation for their intuitive approach. A common feature of statistics textbooks is their organization around mathematical techniques such as linear regression, analysis of variance, and hypothesis testing. By contrast, I bring out the key concepts underlying those techniques, such as variability, correlation, and stratification.

With most books focused on exciting new theories, the work of applied scientists has suffered from general neglect. *Freakonomics* is a notable exception, covering the applied research of the economics professor Steven Levitt. Two books in the finance area also fit the bill: in *The Black Swan*, Nassim Taleb harangues theoreticians of financial mathematics (and other related fields) on their failure in statistical thinking, while in *My Life as a Quant*, Emanuel Derman offers many valuable lessons for financial engineers, the most important of which is that modelers in the social sciences—unlike physicists—should not seek the truth.

Daniel Kahneman summarized his Nobel-prize-winning research on the psychology of judgment, including the distinction between intuition and reasoning, in "Maps of Bounded Rationality: Psychology for Behavioral Economics," published in *American Economic Review*. This body of work has tremendous influence on the development of behavioral economics. The psychologist Richard Nisbett and his cohorts investigated the conditions under which people switch to statistical thinking; see, for example, "The Use of Statistical Heuristics in Everyday Inductive Reasoning," published in *Psychological Review*. In an earlier book, *Judgment Under Uncertainty*, a true classic, Kahneman compiled a list of heuristics that are statistical fallacies.

Slow Merges

The study of waiting has a distinguished history in mathematics and in the discipline of operations research, under the name *queuing theory*. Related research at business schools tends to focus on the evaluation and optimization of real world queuing systems in places such as banks, call centers, and supermarkets. Much of this research focuses on analyzing long-run *average* behavior. Professor Dick Larson at MIT was an early voice in shifting attention from averages to the variability of wait times, as well as the psychology of waiting. His opinion pieces in *Technology Review* and *MIT Sloan Management Review* are worth seeking out. It was David Maister's influential paper "The Psychology of Waiting Times" that set the agenda for studying the psychological aspects of queuing, with the important insight that shortening the perceived waiting time could work just as well as reducing the actual waiting time. The feature articles by Robert Matthews (in *New Scientist*) and Kelly Baron (in *Forbes*), both coincidentally titled "Hurry Up and Wait," depict a range of applications of queuing theory. For the business operations perspective of queuing theory, see *Matching Supply with Demand* by Wharton School professors Gérard Cachon and Christian Terwiesch; for the standard mathematical exposition, see the introductory textbooks by Randolph Hall or Robert Cooper.

The topic of variability is underexposed in statistics books, despite its central importance. The subject is usually filed under *measures of dispersion*—that is to say, median, standard deviation, and percentiles—but the mathematical formulation clouds the practical significance of variability.

The Minnesota Department of Transportation (Mn/DOT) published comprehensive reports on all phases of the "meters shut-off" experiment, including supporting data and implementation details. Cambridge Systematics, the consulting firm hired by Mn/DOT, issued reports on a variety of transportation-related projects, available from the firm's website. The *Minneapolis Star Tribune* employed several top-notch beat writers on transportation, including Jim Foti (known as the Roadguy) and Laurie Blake; the Roadguy blog (http://blogs2.startribune.com/blogs/roadguy) features spirited dialogue between commuters, supplying many quotes for the chapter, including the first opening haiku by Nathan. It was Blake who interviewed Julie Cross, the commuter who experienced variable trip times as a problem of unreliability. Both the *Star Tribune* and *St. Paul Pioneer Press* captured the public reaction before, during, and after the ramp meter experiment, including the quoted comments by Day, Lau, Pawlenty, and Cutler.

Taking advantage of the proximity to an extensive highway system, the renowned University of California, Berkeley, research group known as PATH (Partners for Advanced Transit and Highways) performed groundbreaking work on the freeway congestion paradox, from which they derived the theoretical justification for ramp metering. The article by Chen Chao, Jia Zhanfeng, and Pravin Varaiya, "Causes and Cures of Highway Congestion," is an excellent summary of this impressive body of work. A key to their success must surely be theories built in the service of actual traffic data, not theories for their own sake. Also worth exploring are two reports issued by the Federal Highway Administration: a handbook on ramp management and a primer on traffic bottlenecks.

In *Still Stuck in Traffic*, the economist Anthony Downs wrote the definitive study of traffic congestion, covering both technical and nontechnical aspects of the issue. His principle of "triple convergence" is a winning argument against adding capacity as the final solution to congestion because new capacity will just induce new demand. Downs put forth the provocative thesis that congestion itself is the market's solution to a problem of mismatched supply and demand. National statistics on commuting were taken from Elisabeth Eaves's article "America's Worst Commutes," published in *Forbes*. The American Society of Civil Engineers issues an annual Report Card for America's Infrastructure, which measures road congestion in all fifty states. The engineering community has only recently recognized the importance of managing the reliability (variability) of trip time; see Richard Margiotta's presentation to the National Transportation Operations Coalition, available online, for the state of the art.

There are many more fascinating statistical problems in public transportation. Interested readers should look into high-occupancy-vehicle (HOV) or high occupancy toll (HOT) lanes, clustering of buses and subway trains, Bracss's paradox, the waiting-time paradox, train scheduling, and vehicle routing, among others.

Fast Passes

The Walt Disney Company has earned a sterling reputation for perfecting the guest experience. Some of its industry-leading practices for managing waiting lines were described by Duncan Dickson, Robert Ford, and Bruce Laval in "Managing Real and Virtual Waits in Hospitality and Service Organizations," in which they developed a useful framework for business managers. FastPass is a tremendous hit with Disney fans. The analysis of wait times with and without FastPass came from Allan Jayne Jr.'s "An Unofficial Walt Disney World Web Page," and the tips for using FastPass from Julie Neal's blog, hosted by Amazon.com. Disney fans love to write about their experiences, and these trip reports populate many websites, including MousePlanet.com, DISboards.com and AllEars.net. The various quotations in the chapter were sourced from articles by Steven Ford (in the *Orlando Sentinel*), Marissa Klein (in the *Stanford Daily*), Mark Muckenfuss (in the *Press-Enterprise—Riverside, CA*), and Catherine Newton (in the *Times Union*), and from *The Unofficial Guide to Walt Disney World* by Bob Sehlinger and Len Testa. The second chapter-opening haiku was contributed anonymously to an idiosyncratic fan website called DisneyLies.com, in which the author fact-checks everything about Disney.

The touring plans developed by Len Testa and his associates, including the Ultimate Touring Plan, are found in *The Unofficial Guide* as well as the affiliated TouringPlans.com website. Fans of this irreverent tour guide have snapped up millions of copies of the book. The feat of Waller and Bendeck was recorded on TouringPlans.com. The same website has a write-up of the predictive model, including the relative importance of different factors affecting waiting times. The technical problem Testa addressed belongs to the same family as the notoriously difficult traveling-salesman problem. In brief, it is the search for the quickest route through a list of stops ending back at the origin. A comprehensive reference is *The Traveling Salesman Problem: A Computational Study* by David Applegate, Robert Bixby, Vasek Chvatal, and William Cook.

Bagged Spinach

In January 2000, the *New England Journal of Medicine* published a list of the greatest twentieth-century achievements in medicine,

bringing deserving recognition to the work of statisticians. Epidemiology is much bigger than just investigating outbreaks of diseases.
Kenneth Rothman wrote the standard text on the subject, *Modern
Epidemiology*. Also recommended is the article "Statistical Models
and Shoe Leather," containing keen observations by the statistician
David Freedman. Epidemiologists investigate many types of diseases
beyond food-borne illnesses. Legends abound about the discovery of
the causes of Legionnaires' disease, the Ebola virus, Gulf War syndrome, and so on. These stories of suspense and adventure are well
told in books such as C. J. Peters's *Virus Hunter* and Berton Roue-
ché's *The Medical Detectives*. A wealth of superbly produced materials
is accessible to the public via the Public Health Training Network
of the Centers for Disease Control and Prevention (CDC) and the
Young Epidemiology Scholars program run by the College Board.

The fundamental philosophical debate in epidemiology concerns *causation* and *correlation*. Standard textbooks embed this topic
inside the discussion of *regression*, the workhorse of statistical modeling. More advanced books examine the intertwined subjects of
observational studies and *randomized experiments*. Regarded as the
"gold standard," the randomized experiment is carefully designed
to enable direct and robust attribution of cause to effect. However,
epidemiologists must fall back on the observational study, because
it is unethical to expose people randomly to *E. coli* or other disease
agents. For this type of study, eliciting the cause–effect relationship is achieved by accepting unprovable and sometimes heroic
assumptions—hence the controversy. For a discussion of randomized experiments, see the classic reference *Statistics for Experimenters*
by George Box, Stuart Hunter, and Bill Hunter; for observational
studies, consult the monograph by Paul Rosenbaum and Don
Rubin's *Matched Sampling for Causal Effects* for constructive points
of view; and to comprehend the limitations, study the papers of
David Freedman, who was a professor of statistics at Berkeley.

The ongoing discussion among epidemiologists on the imper-
fection of their statistical methods offers a practical perspective on

causality to supplement the aforementioned academic references. Gary Taubes, a science reporter, offers the best starting point in "Epidemiology Faces Its Limits," published in *Science*, and for more, see commentaries by Erik von Elm (in the *British Medical Journal*), Dimitrios Trichopoulos (in *Sozial und Praventivmedizin*), Sharon Schwartz (in the *International Journal of Epidemiology*), and Kenneth Rothman (in the *American Journal of Public Health*). Alfred Evans gives the subject a book-length treatment in *Causation and Disease*. Steven Levitt and Stephen Dubner describe some riveting case studies in the field of economics; their book *Freakonomics* contains a list of useful references.

The FDA and CDC kept the official record of the *E. coli* investigation of 2006, and the Congressional Research Service published a useful summary. A report by the California Food Emergency Response Team covered the inspection of Californian farms. Local newspapers and media followed events as they unfolded; my sources included the *Los Angeles Times*, the *San Francisco Chronicle*, the *Monterey County (CA) Herald*, *Inside Bay Area*, the *Manitowoc (WI) Herald Times*, the *Appleton (WI) Post-Crescent*, *Lakeshore Health Notes*, radio station WCCO in Minneapolis, and the *Why Files*. In an unusual research report released in 2007, the Food Policy Institute at Rutgers University assessed the media's influence in the crisis. Todd Weiss evaluated the role of computer networks for *Computerworld*. Suzanne Bohan cited Caroline Smith DeWaal's endorsement of the government action in an *Oakland Tribune* article.

Scientific details came from federal and state epidemiologists Michael Lynch, Robert Tauxe, Linda Calvin, Jack Guzewich, Paul Cieslak, and Lorrie King. Kenneth Schulz and David Grimes gave an excellent technical overview of the case–control study in *The Lancet*. Examples of questionnaires used in these studies are available from many state epidemiology departments.

A brief biography of Alexander Langmuir, the founder of the CDC's Epidemic Intelligence Service unit, is given by Jeffrey Koplan and Stephen Thacker in the *American Journal of Epidemiology.*

Bad Score

Commercial credit-scoring algorithms come in many forms, as described in the handsome piece "Statistical Classification Methods in Consumer Credit Scoring: A Review," published in the *Journal of the Royal Statistical Society: Series A*, by David Hand, a statistician at Imperial College London. The innards of credit-scoring models are guarded as commercial secrets. FICO, formerly Fair Isaac Corporation, originated the most widely used credit scores in the United States, known as FICO scores. An excellent presentation called "Credit Scoring 101," created by Fair Isaac, is available at the Federal Trade Commission (FTC) website, www.ftc.gov. Edward Lewis, a former officer of Fair Isaac, wrote a more technical, still readable, but dated reference titled *An Introduction to Credit Scoring.* Bruce Hoadley, also with Fair Isaac, discussed more recent technical innovations, including some practical issues, in the journal *Statistical Science*, while commenting on an important article by Leo Breiman, "Statistical Modeling: The Two Cultures." For a simplified but generally accurate overview of data-mining techniques used in business, see Michael Berry and Gordon Linoff's *Mastering Data Mining.*

The FICO algorithm is typically formulated as a scorecard, as in Lewis's book, or as mathematical equations, as in Hoadley's article. I adopted the simpler form of IF-THEN rules, which is equivalent but more intuitive. In practice, the other formulations are more efficiently implemented. The decision rules cited in Chapter 2 are for illustration only. The rule using debt ratios was mentioned in John Straka's report "A Shift in the Mortgage Landscape: The 1990s Move to Automated Credit Evaluations" in the *Journal of Housing Research*, while the one concerning painters came from Lewis's book.

Many authors have studied the impact of credit scoring on our society; of these efforts, I recommend the book *Paying with Plastic* by David Evans and Richard Schmalensee, and the PBS report on "Credit Scores—What You Should Know About Your Own" by Malgorzata Wozniacka and Snigdha Sen. Although little direct evidence has been published, industry insiders agree on the substantial benefits of credit-scoring models, and their rapid penetration into many industries provides indirect proof. Federal Reserve chairman Alan Greenspan and FTC chairman Timothy Muris made the cited comments at various conferences and hearings.

Consumer advocacy organizations, including the National Consumer Law Center, Center for Economic Justice, and Consumers Union, issued reports critical of credit scoring. The quotation of Representative Steven Wolens was reported by Gary Boulard in *State Legislatures*. Robert Avery at the Federal Reserve organized an innovative study, published in the *Federal Reserve Bulletin*, which concluded that the accuracy of credit report data had only modest impact on consumers. James White's plight was described by Kathy Chu of the *Wall Street Journal*. The piggy-backing scam was detailed in a report by J. W. Elphinstone of the Associated Press.

Claritas, currently owned by Nielsen, is well known among marketing professionals for its proprietary PRIZM segmentation scheme, which divides U.S. households into sixty-six segments with distinct demographic and behavioral characteristics. In his book *The Clustered World*, Michael Weiss presented the profiles of the market segments, as defined by an older generation of PRIZM. Companies use this product to shift from one-size-fits-all marketing to targeted marketing. Customer segmentation typically utilizes cluster analysis, which is a class of statistical models based on correlations. Berry and Linoff's aforementioned book on data mining has a chapter on cluster analysis, which they call "automatic cluster detection."

Item Bank

The seminal reference on DIF analysis remains the volume *Differential Item Functioning* compiled by Paul Holland and Howard Wainer, which covered the influential work conducted by ETS statisticians during the 1980s. The talented staff at ETS publishes a series of research reports, including many papers on DIF; among them is "Revising SAT-Verbal Items to Eliminate Differential Item Functioning" by Ed Curley and Alicia Schmitt, from which I took the sample SAT verbal items. Ed says to look out for new developments, as ETS has launched another cycle of research in this area. Other materials of interest from ETS include a description of its fairness review procedures, a primer on DIF analysis, and summary statistics of historical SAT scores.

Several techniques are currently acceptable for DIF analysis: standardized differences, Mantel–Haenszel statistics, and item-response models. Curley and Schmitt employed the standardization approach. In applying this method to study the group difference by gender, for instance, they computed the correct rate for male examinees as if males had the same mix of ability as females. The group difference is said to have been *controlled* for ability. The other two methods are more mathematically advanced. See the papers "Differential Item Performance and the Mantel–Haenszel Procedure" by Paul Holland and Dorothy Thayer, and "Detection of Differential Item Functioning Using the Parameters of Item Response Models" by David Thissen, Lynne Steinberg, and Howard Wainer.

When an item is found to be unfair to certain groups, the source of inequity frequently defies explanation. The quotation and the anecdote of Lloyd Bond were sourced from his contribution to Holland and Wainer's seminal volume. Some authors use the word *biased* to describe unfair test items and the term *item bias* to describe this field of study. To statisticians, *bias* merely means difference, without the implication of negative intention; I avoided this controversial term altogether, preferring *unfair*. The cumbersome technical term, *differential item functioning*, was coined for a similar reason; it suggests that the unfair items "function" differently from other questions in the test.

DIF analysis requires classifying examinees by their "ability," which also happens to be what the SAT is supposed to measure. Thus, no external source exists for such classification. Clever statisticians tackle this issue by using an internal criterion of ability: an examinee's score on the test after excluding any unfair items. Critics charge that such a metric fails if the test itself fails to measure ability properly. This is a challenge of the validity of standardized testing in general, dressed up as commentary on DIF analysis. The book *Methods for Identifying Biased Test Item*s by psychometricians Gregory Camilli and Lorrie Shepard gives a balanced evaluation of several techniques.

For contemporary views on the Golden Rule settlement, see the special issue (June 1987) of *Educational Measurement*. Nancy Cole, past president of ETS, reviewed the history of fairness reviews in testing in the article "The New Faces of Fairness," published in the *Journal of Educational Measurement*.

Daniel Koretz's *Measuring Up* is a terrific introduction to psychometrics, the application of statistics to educational issues. He devoted a chapter to the achievement gap between black and white students. This phenomenon has been extensively documented and heavily studied. Linda Darling-Hammond distilled the state of our knowledge circa 2007 in the Third Annual Brown Lecture in Education Research, published as "The Flat Earth and Education: How America's Commitment to Equity Will Determine Our Future" in *Educational Researcher*. In his book, Koretz also reviewed the evidence on whether SAT scores predict college GPA. Tia O'Brien wrote about parents in Marin County in the *San Francisco Chronicle*.

Simpson's paradox shows up frequently in practice, and its appearance indicates the presence of group differences that cannot be ignored. In the article "Sex Bias in Graduate Admissions: Data from Berkeley," P. J. Bickel, E. A. Hammel, and J. W. O'Connell supplied a famous example of the statistical paradox. Howard Wainer analyzed several other examples, such as those presented in the article "Two Statistical Paradoxes in the Interpretation of Group Differences."

Risk Pool

For a general introduction to the insurance principle, see Christopher Culp's *The ART of Risk Management* and Chapter 5 of the 2007 *Economic Report of the President*. Both references mention the peculiarities of natural-disaster insurance. For a soft introduction to the mathematics, start with *The Mathematics of Natural Catastrophes* by Gordon Woo, an expert at Risk Management Solutions. Journalist Peter Gosselin reviewed the state of the business of catastrophe insurance in the *Los Angeles Times*. Other useful reading includes *Climate Extremes and Society*, a compilation of recent research; papers by Howard Kunreuther and David Crichton, at the Wharton School of Business and the Aon Benfield UCL Hazard Research Centre (U.K.), respectively; and the presentation by Henry Keeling, CEO of XL Re, to the 2003 Aon Natural Hazards Conference.

Florida newspapers provide excellent accounts of hurricane disasters and comprehensive coverage of insurance-related matters; these include the *St. Petersburg Times*, *Tampa Tribune*, *Palm Beach Post*, and *Sarasota Herald-Tribune*. *Best's Review* analyzes industry news. Bob Hartwig is the chief economist at the Insurance Information Institute, which is funded by the insurance industry, and his colorful presentations archived at the institute's website (www.iii.org) contain much valuable data. Reinsurers, who invest heavily in quantitative modeling, articulate their technical positions in published reports. See especially those written by Munich Re (www.munichre.com) or Swiss Re (www.swissre.com). Ernst

Rauch commented on the accuracy of storm models in a Munich Re report. In 2005, Towers Perrin issued an exhaustive review of Hurricane Katrina's impact on the insurance industry. The Florida Office of Insurance Regulation commissioned several reports on the state of the insurance market.

Statistics affect the insurance business in multiple ways. One key concern is the prediction of expected losses by quantitative-modeling firms. The leading firms that supply insurers with storm models include Risk Management Solutions (located in Newark, New Jersey), AIR Worldwide (Boston), and EQE International (Oakland, California). The *New York Times Magazine* feature article "In Nature's Casino," by Michael Lewis, contained an engaging profile of the entrepreneurs who invented the quantitative-modeling business, explaining how Wall Street benefited by launching markets for catastrophe bonds, which are risky bets on natural disasters not happening during specified periods of time. Catastrophe bonds form a unique class of financial assets that show nearly zero correlation with other assets. The accuracy of catastrophe models has been challenged, but their impact on the industry is unmistakable. Chris Mooney conveyed this material well in his book *Storm World*, particularly the controversy about whether climate change is causing a surge in the intensity or frequency of hurricanes.

The renowned investor Warren Buffett runs a variety of insurance businesses under the Berkshire Hathaway umbrella, and his sage advice on how to stay afloat is sprinkled throughout the chairman's letters to shareholders. In his writings and public comments, Buffett also warned about the growth in financial derivatives and the complexity of interlocking reinsurance contracts.

In recent years, insurers have become quite sophisticated at differentiating between high- and low-risk properties. While the distance from the coast is a clear determinant of potential exposure, actuaries also consider other factors, such as whether customers have taken mitigating measures and whether properties conform to newer building codes. Kunreuther, an insurance expert at the

Wharton School of Business, argues that the industry must move to adopt such risk-based pricing.

The quotations of J. Patrick Rooney came from Lorraine Woellert (in *Business Week*) and J. K. Wall (in the *Indianapolis Business Journal*).

Magic Lassos

Much of the information about the science of polygraphs, including the scientific evaluation of this technology, is drawn from *The Polygraph and Lie Detection*, the 2002 study by the National Academy of Sciences (NAS), an authoritative synthesis of the best available research; and from papers by Stephen Fienberg, professor of statistics at Carnegie Mellon University and the technical director of the NAS study. These sources contain much more on the mathematics of the trade-off and introduce *ROC curves*, a different way of presenting the numbers and the focus of much current research. In a series of articles in the *British Medical Journal*, Douglas Altman and his associates have succinctly introduced the key statistical issues in diagnostic testing, such as sensitivity and specificity, false-positive and false-negative rates, and ROC curves. Both the supporters and adversaries of the polygraph speak loudly: national and local polygraph associations maintain websites, while the opponents gather at AntiPolygraph.org. There exists an earlier study on polygraphs (1983) organized by the Office of Technology Assessment of the U.S. Congress.

The present obsession with data warehouses and data-mining systems in the service of national security will surely fade, as the statistical science of predicting rare events cannot provide sufficient precision to cope with the heavy costs of both false-positive and false-negative mistakes. Better than chance is surely not sufficient. Bruce Schneier's writings—such as those in *Forbes* and *Wired* magazines—are unusual in the mainstream media for their clear-headed grasp of these technical issues. Craig Norris, CEO of Attensity, was cited in the article "'Wholesale' Snooping" by *San Jose Mercury News* reporters Elise Ackerman and K. Oanh Ha. Michael Berry and Gordon Linoff's book, *Mastering Data Mining*, provides a competent introduction to basic data-mining concepts. At Stanford University, the venerable research team of Trevor Hastie, Robert Tibshirani, and Jerome Friedman gives the graduate-school-level treatment of these topics in *The Elements of Statistical Learning*.

The tragic case of Jeff Deskovic highlights the human cost of a false-positive error in real life. Westchester County district attorney Janet DiFiore made the fateful decision to review Deskovic's case, and her office published the authoritative account of it. The *New York Times* followed up with two touching stories, giving us a glimpse into how Deskovic struggled to steer his life back on track after his vindication. Deskovic currently writes a column for the *Westchester Guardian* newspaper and is an activist and motivational speaker. The important work of the Innocence Project, which pursued Deskovic's case as well as hundreds of other wrongful convictions, brings home the reality that perfection is elusive, even though our criminal-justice philosophy condones some false negatives in order to diminish false positives, just as our anti-doping programs do. Professor Saul Kassin has written broadly on false confessions and the extent to which they affect convictions. See, for instance, "False Confessions: Causes, Consequences, and Implications for Reform" and "Confession Evidence: Commonsense Myths and Misconceptions."

Journalist Bill Dedman of MSNBC.com broke the PCASS story in April 2008. The original article, as well as accompanying materials, including the declassified memo by David Thompson at Camp Cropper, can be found on the MSNBC.com website. Surprisingly, few other media outlets picked up the story. The report by Johns Hopkins University scientists John Harris and Allan McQuarrie, titled "The Preliminary Credibility Assessment System Embedded Algorithm Description and Validation Results," contains more details on PCASS, such as how error rates were calibrated. The Wen Ho Lee case was examined thoroughly by Matthew Purdy for the *New York Times* and in Appendix C of the aforementioned 2002 NSA report. A similar case involving another scientist, Dr. Thomas Butler, was reported in depth by the *Cleveland Plain Dealer* in April 2006.

Timid Testers

I use the word *steroids* to refer to performance-enhancing drugs (PEDs) in general; strictly speaking, steroids form a class of PEDs. David Mottram's book *Drugs in Sports* presents a wealth of information about PEDs in sports. Robert Saunders, on his Flies and Bikes blog (www.robertsaunders.org.uk), and Bruce Lynn, in a presentation called "Blood Doping, Erythropoietin, and Altitude Training," described the hematocrit test and the isoelectric focusing test. The World Anti-Doping Agency (WADA) maintains the technical specification of the EPO test, originally developed by Don Caitlin, who leads one of the world's renowned anti-doping laboratories in California.

The statistical analysis of steroid testing follows the textbook approach using conditional probabilities and the famous Bayes' rule, a topic found in every book on probability and statistics. The standard approach focuses on the chance of a chemical false-positive error in the "A" sample; see, for example, Donald Berry's take, published in *Nature*, on the Floyd Landis case. I believe the public cares about the *popular*—not the chemical—false positive. By "popular" false positive, I mean a clean athlete who is falsely accused of doping. This is not the same as a "chemical" false positive, which is a clean blood or urine sample that the testing lab erroneously marks as positive. For a positive "A" sample finding to trigger a popular false positive, the "B" sample must also show abnormal chemistry, the samples must pass additional, more sophisticated lab tests, the process must meet quality-control standards, the result must withstand spirited defense from athletes and lawyers, and the arbitrators must accept cheating as the cause of the positive test. Due to these built-in protections, the chance of a popular false positive can be negligible, even when the rate of a chemical false positive in the "A" sample is not.

Because the error rates of many steroid-testing procedures are not known to the public, textbook analyses make assumptions about the accuracy, usually above 90 percent, which then results in unrealistic positive rates (the sum of true positives and false positives) in the range of 10 to 20 percent. Such rates of positive findings contradict the official records at recent sporting events. For example, Nicolas Brulliard of the *Wall Street Journal* reported that 0.7 percent of tests performed at the 2004 Athens Olympics came back positive; Juliet Macur of the *New York Times* said 2 percent of tests conducted by WADA in 2005 came back positive; and according to Simon Turnbull of *The Independent*, 0.2 percent of tests conducted at the 2008 Beijing Olympics came back positive. Note that these rates put a ceiling on the feasible number of false positives, since a false positive is first and foremost a positive. Experts have no illusion about the false-negative problem: Dr. Charles Yesalis wrote about it in the article "The Strengths and Frailties of Drug Tests," published in the *New York Times*, and Dr. Rasmus Damsgaard's comment about undetected positive samples was mentioned in Matt McGrath's report for BBC News.

Almost all challenges to positive steroid findings in effect confirm the chemical positive, so the real issue of contention concerns competing causes to explain the positive result, pitting cheating against tainted vitamins, spiked drinks, and the like. This latter matter moves us beyond the realm of science into the field of lie detection.

By obtaining a therapeutic-use exemption (TUE) before competing, an athlete is legally allowed to use certain drugs on the banned-substances list, such as anabolic steroids and corticoster-oids. One report disclosed that 60 percent of the 105 cyclists at the 2006 Tour de France received a TUE of one kind or another. More than 100 Major League Baseball players were granted TUEs for attention deficit disorder, according to the official in charge of steroid testing. Most asthmatic Olympic swimmers have obtained TUEs to use certain steroids, and up to half of the elite swimmers suffer from asthma, compared with 5 percent in the general popu-lation, as discussed by Carrie Dahlberg of *The Sacramento Bee*.

The blog Steroid Nation, written by Dr. Gary Gaffney, is unri-valed in delivering timely coverage and insightful commentary on steroids in sports. Mike Lowell's comment about HGH testing was reported by the *Boston Globe*. *Game of Shadows*, the power-ful book by *San Francisco Chronicle* journalists Mark Fainaru-Wada and Lance Williams, provides a riveting behind-the-scenes look at the BALCO investigation, revealing many interlocking stories of competition, greed, jealousy, suspicion, temptation, peer pressure, groupthink, honor, dishonesty, and morality. It will change your perspective on elite athletes. These two investigative journalists deserve praise for their superbly narrated book, which follows a series of scandalous features in their hometown newspaper. Jose Canseco's books, *Juiced* and *Vindicated*, are eccentric and polemical but also thought-provoking and laugh-out-loud funny. Canseco believes that controlled use of steroids is good for sports and good for individuals. In a central chapter of *Vindicated*, he includes tran-scripts of two polygraph examinations that "prove" his truth-telling. The Mitchell Report, published online, named more than eighty baseball players. The testimony of Mark McGwire, Rafael Palmeiro, and Jose Canseco to Congress was widely reported and is readily available online. They no longer play in Major League Baseball. The *New York Daily News* first reported on Rick Ankiel's business with a Florida pharmacy.

Readers should turn to page 173 of *Marion Jones: Life in the Fast Lane* to see her bold-red declaration of innocence years before she finally admitted to doping. It was Sue Mott who made the perceptive remarks about the false negative in the *Daily Telegraph*, the same paper that published Michael Johnson's commentary. Jones retired from track and field. Her coach Trevor Graham stood trial for perjury in 2008 and was later banned for life from track and field. Steve Riddick, another former coach, was convicted in 2006 for his role in a money-laundering scheme involving both Jones and Tim Montgomery. Kelli White was suspended for two years and retired from track; one of the few to admit her mistake and apologize, she later earned an MBA and continues to educate the next generation against doping.

Wikipedia has a nice summary of the multiple doping scandals of the Tour de France, including the list of disgraced former champions. Tyler Hamilton was cited from articles in the *Boston Globe* and *Aspen Times* and his own news release. Arbitrators did not accept his vanishing-twin theory; after serving a two-year ban, he returned to cycling in November 2006 but was suspended again in May 2007 as his name surfaced in the Operacion Puerto drug scandal. In 2009, after failing yet another drug test, Hamilton was served an eight-year suspension, which effectively ended his career. Samuel Abt told the story of Bjarne Riis in the *International Herald Tribune*. Mark Hedden described Riis's awe-inspiring victory at KeysNews.com.

Dick Pound personifies the zealous tester turning over every stone to flush out dopers. A former head of WADA and former Olympic swimmer, he is the larger-than-life figure in the anti-doping movement, and his books include *Inside the Olympics* and *Inside Dope*. Travis Tygart, CEO of the U.S. Anti-Doping Agency, made the clever remark on denials by athletes in an interview with Ferren Christou at the *Daily Peloton*. So many excuses or explanations for positive tests have been proffered by accused athletes that they have been collected and organized as an online quiz at www.sometests.com.

Jet Crashes

Arnold Barnett's research program at Massachusetts Institute of Technology is the most authoritative source on aviation safety. All of the program's work is empirical, developed from historical flight data, and accessible. Statistical testing is their preferred framework. See Barnett's many publications for the analysis of developing-world carriers, USAir, regional carriers, discount airlines, commuter flights, and many other related questions. It was during the Blackett Memorial Lecture in 2001 when Barnett raised the provocative question about fear of flying as a personality disorder.

Barnett's team estimated the risk of fatality to be about 1 in 700,000 for "between-worlds" flights during 1987 and 1996 for both developed-world carriers and their counterparts in the developing world. Imagine a passenger who draws randomly from all scheduled nonstop flights that satisfy her needs; the risk of fatality assesses the likelihood she will perish on the randomly chosen flight. Further, if she were to ride one flight each day, selected at random, it would take 1,900 years before she would be expected to die in a plane crash. This calculation takes into account the probability of the crash in addition to the proportion of passengers who would survive it. What I called "developed world" Barnett labeled the "First World."

Like all disasters, the EgyptAir tragedy received abundant coverage by the media, including the *New York Times*, *Boston Globe*, and *Newsday*. Frank Ahrens used a version of the "Corridor of Conspiracy" table in the *Washington Post*. John Tierney of the *New York Times* cited the study of front-page stories in his paper. Arnold Barnett conducted this study as well. Psychologist Barry Glassner dissected the fear of flying in the *Wall Street Journal* and in Chapter 8 of his book *The Culture of Fear*. The quotation of the anonymous pilot came from the former. The Gallup Poll occasionally reports on the popularity of lotteries and the fear of flying.

Jackpots

The Canadian Broadcasting Corporation broke the story of the Encore lottery fraud in October 2006. The audio recording of the CBC program, titled "Luck of the Draw," is available from their website, where Jeffrey Rosenthal's analysis can also be retrieved. The quotation from the Ontario Convenience Stores Association was reported by Ian Robertson of the *Toronto Sun*. CBC News has reported extensively on the numerous investigations; in particular, Timothy Sawa provided a useful summary of the situation in Western Canada.

Statisticians are not big spenders at casinos, but lotteries and other games of chance are, ironically, their favorite spectator sports. They have studied everything from picking the best numbers to figuring out whether the drawn numbers are truly random. Statistician John Haigh has produced an excellent summary of this research in *Taking Chances*, while William Poundstone's *Fortune's Formula* traced the fortunes of a particular gambling strategy known as Kelly's formula.

Odds and Ends

The terms *probability*, *odds*, and *likelihood* are used interchangeably in my book, as per popular usage, but in technical vocabulary, they have specific and different definitions. The U.S. Census Bureau defines the average day for its American Time Use Survey. Digg is a website (http://digg.com) that ranks online articles by the number of positive responses ("diggs") submitted by Internet readers. Its home page is continuously updated with links to the highest-rated articles.

Index